SIMPLIFIED BOOKKEEPING FOR AUTHORS

BY
GLENN MULLER

COVER DESIGN BY LEILA KIRKCONNELL

SIMPLIFIED BOOKKEEPING FOR AUTHORS

Ver. 1.5

EPUP ISBN 978-1-7772673-2-2

MOBI ISBN 978-1-7772673-1-5

PRINT ISBN 978-1-7772673-0-8

LICENCE NOTES

DISCLAIMER

The information contained within this work is for education and entertainment only. Every attempt has been made to provide accurate, up-to-date, and reliable information. No warranties of any kind are expressed or implied. Readers acknowledge that the author is not engaging in the rendering of any legal, financial, medical, or professional advice. The content of this book has been derived from various sources. Under no circumstances will any legal responsibility or blame be held against the author or publisher for any reparation, damages, or monetary loss due to the information herein, either directly or indirectly. Neither will the publisher or author be held responsible for any errors, omissions, and inaccuracies.

TABLE OF CONTENTS

INTRODUCTION

Let me start by saying 'Congratulations!' - though not necessarily for buying this book (that deserves a thank-you) but for becoming a paid author, and by extension a businessperson. Whether you write fiction or non-fiction, are traditionally or self-published, and have one book or several in the marketplace, the fact that you expect your work to generate revenue puts you on a level that many aspire to yet only a small percentage achieve.

That plateau, however, brings on the new challenge of tracking your business so you know how profitable it is, and to satisfy the demands of your local tax department. Unfortunately, writers and other entrepreneurs are often overwhelmed by the complexities of bookkeeping so they throw all their receipts into a shoebox until the tax man threatens to freeze their bank accounts for not filing. As a professional bookkeeper I hear of this all too often.

Business people tend to be good at what they do, whether they are authors or shop owners or veterinarians, but the bookkeeping segment of a business is a whole other discipline, and after a hard day's work no one wants to sit down and do the math. Except for bookkeepers, which is where I come in. In the light of full-disclosure, I am also a published author. My main genre is the mystery-thriller, and the bane of my existence is not bookkeeping but marketing - we all have an Achilles heel.

Anyway, the point of this book (good - he's finally getting to it) is to provide guidelines to help you record and track the money coming in to your business and the money you are spending to support it, in a way that is simple to understand. I will show you how to keep proper records, and produce reports in a format you can give to your accountant. Yes, you should still have an accountant. Being organized about your finances is one thing. Being smart about them is the next level. Even with my many years of bookkeeping experience I still have an accountant prepare and file my taxes. CPA's know how to work the numbers to minimize the tax payments and maximize the tax refunds. I also believe that filings submitted by accredited accounting firms are audited less frequently than those filed by business owners themselves.

So I don't leave anyone behind, I'm going to assume that beyond having a bank account and writing cheques or using a credit card to pay bills you have done little bookkeeping, and that most accounting terms may not be familiar to you. In fact, we may even get through a few sections before you start to see how everything works together. But don't get discouraged. As you progress through the book, your understanding will improve and I will provide a lot of examples.

I have arranged this guide into several sections:

A section that provides an overview of what bookkeeping is and how it works, with particular attention to how it applies to authors.

A section on common bookkeeping terms that also details the daily, monthly, and yearly tasks that you should do to maintain your books and satisfy the tax agency.

A section on using two different software programs to get you on your way. The programs I have chosen are GnuCash, which is free, and a desktop version of QuickBooks, which you will have to pay for but the price is well worth the extra functionality and ease of use. There are many other good bookkeeping programs available, and you might choose, or already have, something different. That is fine. The nice thing about accounting is that the principles stay the same, not only when using software but also for the type of business that you have. The only difference may be in the various steps required by the software for you to complete a task.

On that note, there is often more than one method of completing a bookkeeping task, so my aim is to show what I have found to be the simplest. Rather than an exhaustive manual, my aim is to provide the basic tools to help you take control of your finances.

While some authors manage to track their finances using spreadsheets, that method though simple does have some drawbacks. Here's just a few:

1) spreadsheets require you to create formulas to make totals or calculate sales tax. If you make an error with these formulae, then you end up with incorrect data.

2) although it is possible to create an invoice template, those invoices will not automatically be stored in a customer file, and you won't get reports on which customers haven't paid

3) as in #2, it is also cumbersome to track vendor bills in a spreadsheet.

4) essentially, by creating several spreadsheets to simulate a set of books, you would just be re-inventing the wheel. The two accounting packages mentioned above will do everything spreadsheets will do and better. They'll ensure you have accurate calculations and give you reports on sales tax and other information that you can give to an accountant for filing your taxes.

Though hiring a bookkeeper or an accountant may sound like an extra expense, just remember that those are business expenses that can be applied against your income, thereby reducing the income tax you have to pay.

Finally, and I may repeat this along the way, if you get stuck and can't find a solution in this book or online, reach out to a bookkeeper in your area. Many do freelance work and are willing to spend an hour or two to help you get set up, or to straighten out a particular problem. And, here, I recommend a bookkeeper over an accountant because, believe it or not, bookkeepers are often better at working with the software and they don't charge nearly as much.

Alright. Now I've given you the basic plot let's delve into the heart of this story.

IT'S ALL ABOUT THE MONEY

Let's face it, seeing your words in print between the covers of a book with your name on is a real joy. And should those book sales and royalties start to trickle into your bank account, then that's even better. We might like reviews but we love money! The reality, though, is that the money can flow both ways. Whereas you should never give an agent money to represent you, or sign a contract with a publisher that requires you to pay them, authors (particularly independent / self-published wordsmiths) still have expenses. Examples range from purchasing computer software, to the writer's workshop fees, to author copies you order from your print-on-demand (POD) service, to the train ticket you bought to attend a book signing event.

No matter which way the money is flowing, the hub of the action is your bank account. As such, if you are serious that writing is a business venture, you should have a dedicated bank account for just your writing-related transactions. There are two main reasons for this:

1) by keeping your business transactions separated from your personal transactions, you'll have an easier time when you have to reconcile your bank statement to your business's books.

2) it demonstrates to the tax department that your writing is a business - and not just a hobby. This makes it easier for them to accept your expenses, particularly if you happen to show a loss for the year.

Acknowledging that the bank account is the hub of all transactions will make it easier for you to determine how to record each entry into your books. If you are not already familiar with the bookkeeping terms, `Debit` and `Credit`, you soon will be. I am going to show you the basics of double-entry bookkeeping, which basically means there are two sides to every transaction - a `Debit` amount and a `Credit` amount.

Two examples:

1) You buy a ream of paper for your printer - say $5. In your books you would `Credit` your Bank account $5 and `Debit` your Office Supplies account $5.

2) You receive a royalty payment from one of your online distributors - $85. In your books you would `Debit` your bank account $85 and `Credit` your Royalty Revenue account $85.

Simply put, **if money comes out of your bank then you post it as a `Credit`. If money goes into your bank then you post it as a `Debit`.** Once you know that the bank entry will be a `Debit` or `Credit` then the other side of the entry (what the money is for) will in most cases be the opposite.

When setting up your books, you will need to create several accounts. Let's move on to the next section; *It's also about organization*, to learn about these accounts.

IT'S ALSO ABOUT ORGANIZATION

Most successful authors schedule time each day to write. They treat it like any other job. The act of writing, though, does not get recorded in the bookkeeping. It's all the other stuff like buying office supplies, paying for advertising, receiving royalties, and other such transactions that happen almost daily that need to be recorded. However, you don't have to schedule time each and every day for this. An hour or so, every couple of weeks will probably be sufficient. Even with my bookkeeping business, apart from invoicing, I only find it necessary to record my transactions about twice a month. I usually enter the transactions for the first half of the month just after the 15th, and will record the transactions for the second half of the month in the first few days of the next month. The important thing is to do it regularly.

A big advantage of keeping up with your bookkeeping is that you stay current on your bank and credit card balances, which helps to avoid overdrafts. It also helps you to budget, and can show you which of your products is generating the most income. It also keeps the sessions fairly short so we can get back to our writing. Nothing distracts an author more than worrying about whether they missed paying a bill, or if they'll have to come up with money to pay the tax man. With that off your mind only a blank page and a little inspiration will stand between you and your next great publication.

So, now that you've organized your time, let's examine how financial books are organized.

To set up your "books" you first need to create a Chart of Accounts. This is a set of accounts that represent what you own; who you owe; where your money comes from; and where it is spent. These accounts are organized into a list that has five main categories:

ASSETS

These accounts represent the value of things that your business owns, like the money in your business bank account; office equipment; the stock of books in your basement that you hope to sell (also known as inventory).

Another important asset account is called Accounts Receivable. This is money that is owed to you. Perhaps you did some ghost-writing for a client and sent them an invoice which they have not yet paid. The amount of that invoice is considered an asset.

Asset account amounts are usually entered as `Debits`. Assets can be split into two categories: Current Assets, which are accounts where the value fluctuates, sometimes day to day; and Fixed Assets, which are usually high-value items like equipment.

LIABILITIES

These accounts represent amounts that your business owes, like your credit card balance, loans from a bank or other source, sales tax collected that you haven't yet remitted to the tax agency.

Accounts Payable is an important liability account that represents the money you owe to your vendors. You may have received an invoice from a cover designer. Until you pay that bill, the amount sits in the Accounts Payable account.

Changes to Liability accounts are usually entered as `Credits`. Liabilities can also be split into two categories: *Current Liabilities*, which are debts you expect to pay within a year; and *Long-term Liabilities*, which are larger debts that may take more than a year to pay back.

Here are a couple of Journal Entries that involve liability accounts:

Let's say a furniture store was offering a low-interest rate on a "buy-now / pay-later" promotion, so you decide to splash out on new office furniture; desk, chair, lamps, bookshelves - all mahogany - Total $1,000 + $100 sales tax. So, you sign an agreement that states you will pay monthly instalments for the next 12 months, with a 6% annual interest rate. Here's the math:

\$1,000 (cost) + \$100 (tax) + \$66 (interest) = \$1,166.00

\$1,166.00 divided by 12 months = 11 payments of \$97.16 and 1 payment of \$97.24

Here is what the Journal Entry for the purchase would look like:

Account	Debit	Credit	Memo
Furniture & Equipment	1000.00		Office furniture
Sales Tax Payable	100.00		Office furniture
Interest Expense	66.00		Office furniture
Furniture Store Liability		1166.00	Office furniture

Now, when you make your monthly payments, the journal entry would look like this:

Account	Debit	Credit	Memo
Bank Chequing Account		97.16	Monthly payment
Furniture Store Liability	97.16		Monthly payment

The `Debit` of \$97.16 will be applied each month against the original `Credit` of \$1,166.00 until your 12th payment of \$97.24 finally reduces the liability to \$0.00.

Another type of liability is the *Short-term Loan*. You may borrow some money, or perhaps loan the business some money from your own savings. Again, you would set up a Liability account for each lender.

Note - when you are lending your business money, this is not to be confused with investing in your business (see the section below on Equity - Owner's Equity). An investment means you do not expect the business to pay you back. A loan means that you do expect repayment, at some point, from the business.

EQUITY

Every business needs an investment of some sort, in the beginning. Even if all you have done so far is write your first manuscript, by hand, on a pad of paper, you have made the investment of a pen ($1.25) and a pad ($1.75). Most likely, though, you will open a bank account and deposit an amount (say, $250.00) of your own money. This is equity that you have put into the business. Changes to Equity accounts are usually entered as `Credits`.

There are a number of equity accounts that you need in your Chart of Accounts. They are Opening Balance / Retained Earnings / Owner's Equity / Owner's Draw - or, if you have set up your business as a Partnership or Corporation, then you will have Shareholder's Equity instead of Owner's Equity. A brief explanation of these accounts follows:

Equity - Opening Balance:

One of the first things you will record is the state of your business as of the first day of your bookkeeping. You will list Assets like the bank balance, estimated current value of your equipment, etc.; Liabilities like any funds loaned to you for your business, or credit card amounts on anything you had purchased for your business prior to opening day; Equity such as money you invested; and Expenses like the value of any office supplies. The sum of these amounts will be considered your Opening Balance which is essentially what your business is worth on day one. We'll look at this in more detail later on.

Note - When making the Opening Balance entries the date will be the day before the start of your fiscal year. So, if your fiscal year starts on January 1st. then your Opening Balance entries will be dated December 31st. of the previous year. This is so you will have an accurate record of transactions that happened only during the fiscal year, itself. The opening balances should also be the very first journal entry you will make in your program.

***Equity* - Retained Earnings:**

At the end of your Fiscal Year (365 days since the starting calendar date of your business) the difference between your income and expenses for the year will determine if you have made a profit or experienced a loss. Either way, the amount of that difference is posted to the Retained Earnings account. As each year ends, the Retained Earnings account will show a cumulative record of how your business has performed from day one all the way up to the date of the most recent year-end adjustment.

***Equity* - Owner's Equity:**

Amounts posted to this account represent any personal funds that you have invested in the business, or the value of any equipment or property that you personally have donated to the business. These are amounts that you do not expect to be repaid.

Here is an example: You've got a book signing lined up at a popular book fair, so you order a batch of books from your printer (Cost $500), but you've only got $200 in your business bank account. So, from your own piggy bank you deposit another $300 into your business bank account. The entry would look like this:

Account	Debit	Credit
Bank Chequing (Asset account)	300.00	
Owner's Equity (Equity Account)		300.00

If you are donating equipment to your business, like a computer that you estimate is worth $450, then the entry would look like this:

Account	Debit	Credit
Equipment (Asset account)	450.00	
Owner's Equity (Equity Account)		450.00

Equity - Owner's Draw:

As a sole proprietor, you will not get a paycheque. If you want to be paid then you must draw money from the business. As the owner, it is up to you how much you take, and how often you do this.

Note - this is one equity account where entries are listed as `Debits`.

Here's an example: The food cupboard is empty so you "pay yourself" $150.00 with which to buy groceries. The entry would look like this:

Account	Debit	Credit
Bank Chequing (Asset account)		150.00
Owner's Draw (Equity account)	150.00	

The above transactions nicely illustrate that money going into the bank is a `Debit` and money coming out of the bank is recorded as a `Credit`. Remember, if you know what is happening to the bank account, you can figure out on which side the other entry goes.

INCOME

The income accounts represent money that comes to your business from outside sources. Hopefully, most of that will be from your book sales or royalties though you may earn interest income on your bank balance. The income accounts we will start with are as follows:

Book Royalties - sales from a distributor where you receive a portion of the selling price.

Book Sales - from your own sales where you get 100% of the sale amount.

Interest Income - likely from having such a large balance in your chequing account.

Other Income - a good account to have for unforeseen deposits like signing bonuses or cash awards.

Reimbursed Expenses - perhaps you shipped out books and charged the customer postage (and, yes, you can charge more than you spend).

Note - if you get a refund from a vendor, it is not listed as income. The refund amount would be posted to the original expense you are getting the refund for.

Entries to Income accounts are usually `Credits`. Here is an example:

Account	Debit	Credit
Bank Chequing (Asset account)	39.50	
Book Royalties (Income account)		39.50

You can see it follows the rule of thumb where money going into the bank is always a `Debit`, and the other side is a `Credit`.

EXPENSES

With a few exceptions, expenses are the amounts you pay to run your business. Fortunately, writers generally have very little physical "overhead" to worry about. We don't have to keep a factory running, or even a bricks and mortar store for that matter. Still, we're going to need equipment and office supplies, we'll likely pay for some advertising and for author copies of our book. Perhaps you'll pay to have a cover made, or for an editor to polish your chapters. Maybe you took a taxi to a book signing, or bought lunch for your agent. All of these cash outlays are expenses that you can use to lower your taxes at the end of the year. Even the purchase price of this book can claimed. How about that!

The important thing is that you must have a receipt for every expense whether it is an invoice from the computer repair shop, or a parking lot stub. The tax agency will not allow any expense that isn't backed up with a receipt, so keep everything and claim everything.

The main exception to using an expense to lower your tax payables is the interest (finance) charged for late payment on government remittances. These might be penalty charges for overdue income tax, or perhaps you were late paying a property tax bill and got dinged with interest. You can still pay them from your business bank account, and as such will still record them in the Ineligible Interest account, but because they are ineligible they cannot be used to lower your taxes.

Another expense that can't be claimed is a parking ticket (not to be confused with a parking stub) or other such fine.

Expenses are generally posted as `Debit` entries. Here is an example:

You pay an editor $1500.00 to put the final polish on your new book, *The Secret Life of Mary Poppins.*

Account	Debit	Credit
Bank Chequing (Asset account)		1500.00
Outside Services (Expense account)	1500.00	

Or, perhaps, you used your credit card to pay the editor:

Account	Debit	Credit
Credit Card (Liability account)		1500.00
Outside Services (Expense account)	1500.00	

Okay, now that we're familiar with the main categories used to organize our transactions let's get acquainted with some of the accounting terminology.

COMMON TERMS

Like other disciplines, accounting has it's own terms and phrases.. Let's get you familiar with some of the more common bookkeeping jargon.

SOLE PROPRIETORSHIPS, PARTNERSHIPS, CORPORATIONS

There are three basic types of business enterprise: *Sole Proprietorship, Partnership*, and *Corporation*. If you are consistently making six figures or more from your published books, I expect your accountant would have advised you to incorporate. The cost to do this, though, can run into the thousands. Most of us, however, can manage by registering as sole proprietors and getting a business number so we can collect, claim, and remit sales tax (more on this later). An Internet search on your local tax department's website should provide details and cost for this.

As a *Sole Proprietor*, you file your business income as part of your personal income tax. If you work out of your home, as many writers do, then you will also be able to claim a portion of your home and vehicle expenses - usually on a separate tax form that gets included with your filing. A *Partnership* is very similar, with the partners having some agreement as to investment, sharing of expenses, and taking of profits. The disadvantage is that the owners of sole proprietorships or partnerships are on the hook for any losses the business may incur. However, since you probably won't have a lot of overhead, and hopefully, you don't go crazy on giant billboards or paying for celebrity endorsements, your outlay shouldn't be so much that you lose sleep.

If your business is a *Corporation*, then any loss the business incurs is limited to the assets of the business. Since your house is most likely listed in your name (not listed as a business asset), then you won't lose your home when that movie you decided to produce gets shut down due to a pandemic (could happen).

Another difference is that if you incorporate you can give yourself a paycheque. The upside is that any wages are considered an expense which can be used to reduce your income, which lowers your tax debt. The downside of issuing a paycheque is that you will then have to pay employment source deductions to the tax department.

For now, to keep your introduction to bookkeeping on the simplified side, we will concentrate mainly on a sole proprietorship.

FISCAL YEAR

The success of a business is generally measured by how much profit it makes over the course of a year. The start and end of the year will always be on the same dates covering a period of twelve months. For sole proprietors, the fiscal year is the same as the calendar year - January 1st to December 31st.

This also keeps things simple when filing your income taxes.

TRANSACTION

A transaction can be the exchange of something of value, for example a reader gives you cash and you give them a book. A transaction may also represent a change in value. For example, you could buy a new laptop computer but each year it will devalue. The transaction in this case would record the amount (a percentage of the original cost) that the laptop has devalued.

ENTRY

The recording of a transaction.

POST

To post an entry means to commit the transaction to your books. Just like you save your work when typing a chapter in Word or Scrivener, or whatever you use, to 'Post' an entry means you are satisfied with what you have entered and want to save it.

Depending on the type of transaction, and the software you use, you may or may not be able to change a transaction once you have posted it. If you do change a transaction, then you will have to post (save) it again.

JOURNAL ENTRY (JE)

Sometimes called a General Journal Entry, this is a standard way of recording transactions. When you make a journal entry in your computer software the screen will look like a spreadsheet with the following columns:

`Account | Debit | Credit | Memo` - although you don't always have to fill in the memo section, it does help to remind you what the entry is for. See an example below in the explanation for `Debits` and `Credits`.

Note - most bookkeeping software programs have nice interfaces for entering invoices, paying bills, recording customer payments, etc. that handle the `Debits` *and* `Credits` *for you. Let's say you had a computer fixed and paid the repair shop with a cheque. In your program you would fill out something that looked like a cheque, and the software would automatically post the cost, the tax, and the payment to the correct accounts.*

DEBIT AND CREDIT

There are two sides to every transaction, a `Debit` side and a `Credit` side. Although a transaction may involve more than two accounts, when totalled up the `Debits` should always equal the `Credits`.

Here is an example;

You spend $49.00 on some toner for your printer. The entry would be Debit your Office Supplies account $49.00 | Credit your Bank Chequing account $49.00.

Now, there was probably sales tax on that $49.00. Where I live it is 13% ($6.37) so the total purchase would be $55.37. In that case, your entry would look like this:

Account	Debit	Credit	Memo
Office Supplies	49.00		printer toner
Sales Tax Payable	6.37		tax on toner
Bank Chequing		55.37	toner purchase
	55.37	55.37	

So you see that the Debits equal the Credits.

In the section titled *It's also about organization*, we saw how Assets, Liabilities, Equity, Income, Expenses, and their associated accounts normally require either a Debit entry or a Credit entry (but not always). Until you get familiar with the nature of the accounts it can be a little confusing but I'll continue to give examples to help you along.

The term Credit can also be used to describe an allowance you either receive from a vendor or give to a customer, usually for goods that were incorrect, damaged, or not received. The opposite of a bill or invoice, these notices can also be called *Credit Notes*.

RECONCILIATION

Your bookkeeping should be an accurate reflection of what is happening in the real world where your finances are concerned. The 'real world' in this case is represented by your bank and credit card statements which are usually issued by your bank and credit card company once a month. When you get these statements you should do a reconciliation, which means compare the transactions listed on the statements with the entries you have posted to your bank and credit card accounts in your software. Your program will have a nice little reconciliation routine for checking off the entries that match.

Just as on your statements, you will enter the balance as of the first day of the statement, and the balance as of the last day of the statement, and when you have finished matching everything up the difference between the start and finishing balances should show $0.00. If not, perhaps you missed recording a purchase, or perhaps the bank made a mistake - it happens.

PAYABLE

A payable is any amount you owe for a product or service you have received but not yet paid for. An example would be a bill from a graphic designer who did the cover art for your book. You have the artwork but have not paid for it.

RECEIVABLE

A receivable is any amount that is owed to you for a product or service that you have provided. Perhaps you did some editing for a budding author. You sent them an invoice for $150 but they have not yet sent you a cheque.

PROFIT

If you sold one of your books for $20.00, but it cost you $6.00 to have it printed, then the basic profit would be $14.00. Of course there are other 'hidden' costs to running a business but for now we'll just keep it simple.

LOSS

Don't be surprised if in your first year as a professional author you incur a loss; meaning that over the year you actually had more expenses than you did sales. It takes some investment to start a business and expenses always come before sales. Just have faith in your writing and be smart about how you spend your money.

GROSS INCOME VS NET INCOME

You will find these two amounts on your *Income Statement* reports. Gross Income is all of the money that you have earned in a certain period (not counting taxes on sales). Net Income is the Gross Income minus all of your Expenses for the same period.

When filing taxes, you will often have to report your Gross Income, although you'll likely pay tax on an amount that is closer to, if not exactly, your Net Income.

BAD DEBT / WRITE-OFF

One of the realities of running a business is that we don't always get paid for our work. If you can always get money in advance then you won't have to worry about that. However, if you provide a service like ghost-writing, and invoice when the job is complete, then there are any number of reasons why a customer may not pay you.

Once it is obvious that your chances of collecting from the customer are slim to none, then you need to write-off the amount. Whatever the unpaid amount is, you will need to separate the appropriate amount of sales tax. For example; if the original invoice was for $88.00 ($80 for services plus $8.00 for the 10% sales tax) then you would post $80.00 to the Bad Debt account and $8.00 to the Sales Tax Payable account. The journal entry would look like this:

Account	Debit	Credit	Memo
Accounts Receivable		88.00	bad debt-Smith inv. 211
Sales Tax Payable	8.00		bad debt-Smith inv. 211
Bad Debt	80.00		bad debt-Smith inv. 211
	88.00	88.00	

If the customer paid part of the invoice, but not the rest, then you would adjust the bad debt / sales tax portions accordingly to equal the unpaid amount.

DUE ON RECEIPT VS NET 30 DAYS

Payment terms specify the time period given for the payment of a bill or invoice. The three most common terms are *Due On Receipt*, *Net 10 Days*, and *Net 30 Days*. These are used to prompt the customer to pay in a reasonable amount of time. In many cases larger companies will also charge interest on unpaid amounts after the term has expired.

Just like your suppliers give you terms, you can do the same with your customers. As an author, I have found little need to charge interest, however, all of my invoices state that payment is *Due On Receipt*. If it takes a week (or month with large distributors) for the money to get to me then I can live with that, but in my experience as a bookkeeper I have found that giving *Net 30 Days* leads customers to think they don't have to pay until at least 30 days has gone by - and the staler an invoice gets, the harder it is to collect on.

Since selling to friends and at book signings is generally an immediate complete transaction, *Due On Receipt* is a given.

OUT OF POCKET

Out of pocket means that you, or someone working for you, spent their own money on a business purchase. This is recorded as a liability since, at some point, the business will have to reimburse the purchaser. In most cases, the business owner (you) will be out of pocket, and so the entry would post to the Owed To Owner liability account. We'll be look at this account in more detail, later on.

CASH-BASED VS ACCRUAL ACCOUNTING

When you are setting up your bookkeeping program, it may ask if you want to set up for *Cash-Based* or *Accrual* accounting. I always tell my clients to use *Accrual-based* accounting, unless they are operating a lemonade stand on their front lawn where everything is paid for immediately, in cash.

The main difference is that most businesses don't always exchange money at the time a sale or an expense is realized. It is not unusual to receive a service or make a sale in one month but not have the bill paid until the next. Accrual accounting recognizes the sale (if not the payment) at the moment it happens. This gives a more accurate picture of your business, particularly if you have inventory (if you keep a stock of your books then you have inventory).

Also, for tax reasons, the tax agency recognizes sales tax as of the date on the invoice or vendor bill - not when that invoice or bill got paid.

SALES TAXES - RECORDING, CALCULATING, FILING

Because your local tax agency will look carefully at your business when it comes to sales tax, I felt the topic should have its own section. Depending on your situation, you may be required to report your sales tax activity either annually (once a year), quarterly (every three months), or monthly. Having said that, sometimes you do not have to report at all.

While I cannot speak for all tax agencies, I know that the Canada Revenue Agency (CRA) has a maximum income limit of $30,000.00 for business owners who do not want to collect or pay sales tax. In other words, if you consistently make less than $30,000.00 selling your product each year, then you do not have to charge sale tax on your books and services. Nor do you have to file sales tax reports. Before you go this route, however, make sure you check the rules for your particular region.

Although not collecting and not reporting sales tax sounds like a convenience for those with low sales, I recommend AGAINST going this route for a number of reasons:

Reason One: If you are not going to charge sales tax on your products and services, neither can you claim the sales tax you paid on your purchases. This is particularly important in your first year of business when you will likely have more purchases than sales. You will keep track of all sales tax you collect, and all sales tax you pay out, in the Sales Tax Payable account. Since this is a liability account, if the balance is in the `Credit` column then you owe that amount to the tax agency. But, if the balance is in the `Debit` column then the tax agency owes you that amount. And they will send you a refund.

Reason Two: Think positively - think big. Perhaps you have just started seeing some income from the sale of your books. A few paperbacks sold at a book fair, some sold to friends and relatives, small royalties trickling in from Amazon. But we should always set our sights higher and expect that someday we will have a fan-base that is clamouring for the next book in our gothic horror series, or the next instalment of *Captured by Pirates*.

Reason Three: When you charge sales tax on your products and services, your customers see you as a professional, not just as someone with a little writing hobby. They will take your work more seriously and, as they say in Hollywood, image is everything.

Reason Four: Although it sounds like you will have to pay the tax agency money that you collected, just remember that the sales tax was never your money to begin with. It is an amount the customer paid you to be passed on to the government. You are just the conduit in that transaction, and some tax agencies will even let you keep a small percentage of what you collect.

Reason Five: Whether you report sales tax, or not, you will still have to pay sales tax every time you make a purchase. You may as well get that back. It's money, baby! Don't leave anything on the table.

Reason Six: Charging, recording, calculating, and filing sales tax is not hard. I'll show you how.

Once you have set up your software, whenever you record a sale or a purchase, the program will automatically post the sales tax to the Sales Tax Payable* liability account. *Sales Tax Payable is a generic term I'll use to represent whatever the tax is called in your region. Often, the software will automatically create these accounts for you, and can be set up to calculate the tax on transactions.

The software will also allow you to easily run a report on the Sales Tax Payable account for a given period. If the program allows you to export the report to an Excel spreadsheet, I suggest you do so. If not, just print out the report.

Now, whether is printed out or exported to a spreadsheet, you'll need to look carefully at the amounts posted in the `Debit` and `Credit` columns. **Only amounts pertaining to purchases you've made should be in the `Debit` column, and only amounts pertaining to customer sales should be in the `Credit` column.**

However, if you gave a refund to a customer, then the sales tax amount on that refund will appear in the `Debit` column. Or, if you took something back to a store and the store issued you a refund, when you post that refund in your program it will post the sales tax portion to the `Credit` column.

Those refund amounts will have to be moved into the other column. But don't do it in the program, just do it manually on the printed report, or in the spreadsheet. And when you move the amounts into the other column, make them **negative** amounts. See the examples below.

Example 1 - how the report initially looks (I have made **bold** the amounts on the wrong side):

Sales Tax Payable Report for Jan 1, 2020 to Mar 31, 2020

(*this report just shows the sales tax from the transactions*)

Date	Transaction	Debit	Credit	Memo
01/15/20	Book Sale		1.00	Misc. customer
01/19/20	Book Sale		3.00	Misc. customer
01/20/20	Purchase	2.59		Printer paper
01/30/20	Book Sale		2.00	Misc. customer
02/06/20	Purchase	6.88		Toner cartridge
02/10/20	Book Sale	**1.00**		**Refund-torn cover**
02/11/20	Purchase	3.26		Mailing envelopes
02/12/20	Purchase		**6.88**	**Wrong toner-Returned**
02/12/20	Purchase	7.64		Toner cartridge
03/17/20	Book Sale		8.00	Cambridge Book Fair
03/18/20	Purchase	4.39		Computer repair
	Report Totals	25.76	20.88	

Example 2 - how the report should look (I have made **bold** the corrections):

Sales Tax Payable Report for Jan 01, 2020 to Mar 31, 2020

(**this report just shows the* *sales tax* *from the transactions*)

Date	Transaction	Debit	Credit	Memo
01/15/20	Book Sale		1.00	Misc. customer
01/19/20	Book Sale		3.00	Misc. customer
01/20/20	Purchase	2.59		Printer paper
01/30/20	Book Sale		2.00	Misc. customer
02/06/20	Purchase	6.88		Toner cartridge
02/10/20	Book Sale		**-1.00**	**Refund-torn cover**
02/11/20	Purchase	3.26		Mailing envelopes
02/12/20	Purchase	**-6.88**		**Wrong toner-Returned**
02/12/20	Purchase	7.64		Toner cartridge
03/17/20	Book Sale		8.00	Cambridge Book Fair
03/18/20	Purchase	4.39		Computer repair
	Report Totals	17.88	13.00	

Having corrected our *Sales Tax Payable Report* (I repeat, do manually only - don't try to change it in the program), we can see that we spent $17.88 in sales tax on purchases, and collected $13.00 in sales tax from our customers. In this case, we can claim a $4.88 refund from the tax agency.

Now, you might say that is the same result that you would get with the original report; however, the tax agency will often compare your *sales income* total to the amount of *sales tax* you collected, so we want that percentage to be as close to the prescribed tax rate as possible.

Note - if you have previously filed for a prior period, and either paid an amount owing or received a refund from the tax agency, that payment or refund needs to be recorded as a `Debit` *(refund) or* `Credit` *(payment) in the* Bank *account, and a* `Debit` *(payment) or* `Credit` *(refund) to the* Sales Tax Payable *account.*

*Those refund or payment amounts will then appear in your Sales Tax Payable report - **it is important that you do not include those amounts in the totals for your next filing.** Those particular amounts simply cancel the balance of the last report, and should have no influence on the totals of the new report. Again, you will manually exclude those amounts on your working paper or spreadsheet - don't remove them in the program.*

Before you file your claim, you will need to run an *Income Statement* report for the period. The amount you will file will be the `Gross Income Earned` (before expenses). You will also need to have your Business Number / Sales Tax Number or ID handy.

Personally, my current financial situation requires that I file every three months, but it doesn't take me long to do so; perhaps five minutes to run the reports and adjust any refunds, and another five minutes to go online to the tax agency website and input the numbers. If I owe money, my tax agency's website also has a link where I can schedule a direct payment from my bank.

One further point about sales taxes. While you are checking your local tax agency's website to find out the sales tax in your region, you should look specifically for sales tax on books. Where I live the sales tax on goods and services is 13% - however, on books it is only 5%. Also, where you ship your books may, or may not, have an applicable tax. For example, I live in Canada, so if you lived in the USA and ordered a book from me, directly, I would not be able to charge you any tax at all. Having said that, tax may still be applied by Customs when it crosses the border, but that would be paid by the purchaser and would not affect the seller.

HOME OFFICE EXPENSES

Those of us that don't have a separate building, such as a rented space that we use for our business, will most likely work out of a home office. As such, we can claim a portion of our home expenses such as heat, electricity, water, insurance, some repairs, etc. to reduce our tax debt at the end of the fiscal year.

To meet the requirements for tax purposes, a home office must be a dedicated space (ideally a room) that is only used for your business. However large or small the space, calculate the portion of the interior of your house that this space occupies. For example, if your home has ten rooms and you use one of them for an office, then the home office portion would be 10%. A claim of 10 - 15% would be considered reasonable.

If you have a mortgage then a portion of the mortgage interest can be claimed. If you rent your living space, then you can claim a portion of the rent.

For Sole Proprietors, a portion of your vehicle costs are also claimable under home office expenses. Vehicle costs are fuel, repairs and maintenance, insurance, and if you have a lease then the monthly lease payments. Also, if you took out a loan to pay for the vehicle you can claim some of the interest on the loan (not the loan itself).

If your business is a Corporation, then you can probably list your vehicle in your books as an Asset, and depreciate a portion of its value each year, along with posting applicable expenses right in your bookkeeping software.

Note - it's a good idea to discuss this with your accountant.

To be able to claim vehicle expenses, you must keep a mileage log. I have a little notebook that I keep in the car. I record the odometer reading at **the beginning of the year** - (ie) 21,705 then whenever I drive anywhere for business purposes, and this can be to the office supply store, to visit bookshops, to go to book fairs, any travel for research, etc., I record the odometer reading **at the start of the trip** which could be 22,369 and then record the reading **at the end of the trip**, say 22,398.

In this example I travelled (22398 - 22369) 29 miles or kilometers. I will eventually record all these trips in a spreadsheet that looks something like this:

Year: 2020 Start-Jan 01 = 21705 End-Dec 31 = 24805

Date	From	To	Start	End	TripTotal
(these are all round trips - home-destination-home)					
01/15/20	Home	Staples	21904	21926	22
02/13/20	Home	Bob's Bookshop	21957	21989	32
04/14/20	Home	Town Library	21286	21299	13
06/24/20	Home	Book Tour	21855	22503	648
11/05/20	Home	Fall Book Fair	23869	23899	30

At the end of the year I will note the odometer reading (24,805) and that will give me the total mileage travelled for the year (24805 - 21705), in this case 3150 kilometers. Then I will add up the mileage for all the business trips, say it was 745 kilometers. Then I can figure out the percentage of travel that was for business. Here's the math:

745 / 3150 = 0.23650793

So your calculator might give you this great long number. Just take the first three digits after the decimal point (236) and round it up to 24. This tells us that of all the driving around you did during the year, 24% of it was for business. Now that you know this, you can claim **24%** of all your **vehicle expenses** along with your home office expense claim.

*Note - parking tickets are NOT an expense you can claim. However, **100%** of parking stubs, toll road fees, or weekend car rentals (and fuel used in such) can all be claimed, and these CAN be entered into your bookkeeping program.*

Here is an example of how to calculate home office expenses.

Note - I'm just going to show the totals for the year.

Expense	Cost	Tax	Office%	% Cost	% Tax
Electricity	880.00	88.00	10%	88.00	8.00
Heating	1100.00	110.00	10%	110.00	11.00
Water	500.00	0.00	10%	50.00	0.00
Internet	720.00	72.00	50%	360.00	36.00
Home Insurance	1200.00	0.00	10%	120.00	0.00
Home Maintenance	918.50	91.85	10%	91.85	9.19
Mortgage Interest	600.00	0.00	10%	60.00	0.00
Property Taxes	2850.00	0.00	10%	285.00	0.00
Vehicle Lease	4134.00	413.40	24%	992.16	99.22
Vehicle Fuel	1554.00	155.40	24%	372.96	37.30
Veh. Maintenance	740.00	74.00	24%	177.60	17.76
		Totals to claim		**2707.57**	**218.47**

I would record all of this in a spreadsheet (not your bookkeeping program) then give it to my accountant. Home expenses are input onto a separate form when filing your income taxes.

In the above example I used 10% for the sales tax rate. You will need to put in the actual amounts, of course, keeping in mind that some things are not taxed (or the tax is not claimable - ask your accountant). You will also have noticed that I used 24% as per the vehicle mileage calculation we did (above), and I put the internet portion as 50%. Again, you will have to work out for yourself exactly what these amounts and percentages really are for your situation.

THE CHART OF ACCOUNTS

Apart from keeping your transactions organized, the Chart of Accounts gives you some flexibility as to how detailed you want your financial reports. For example, you may have several different methods of publicizing your work. You could pay for ads on Facebook, or Amazon, or BookBub. You could have flyers printed, or take out space in a newspaper or magazine. You could pay for exposure on a book review site, or for a booth at a book fair. My point, here, is that you can list all of these expenditures in just one account called Advertising or Promotion, or you can have an account for each kind of publicity expense. It all depends on how detailed you want to be.

Below, I will give you what I feel are the basic accounts you should start with, then I'll provide a brief explanation of each:

I'll just remind you that the Chart of Accounts is organized into five main categories, and they generally appear in this order:

Asset, Liability, Equity, Income, Expense.

Checking Account (or Chequing account, if you prefer - just Edit the name)

Savings Account

PayPal or similar (Optional)

Petty Cash

Accounts Receivable

Furniture & Equipment

Accum. Depr. Equip. & Furn.

Inventory

Credit Card

Owed to Owner

Sales Tax Payable

Accounts Payable

Opening Balances

Retained Earnings

Owner's Equity

Owner's Draw

Book Royalties

Book Sales

Interest Income

Other Income

Reimbursed Expenses

Advertising & Promotion

Bank / Credit Card Fees

Bank / Credit Card Interest

Cost of Goods Sold

Depreciation

Donations

Dues and Subscriptions

Education / Workshops

Equipment Rental

Exchange Gain or Loss

Interest - Ineligible

Internet Expense

Licenses and Permits

Meals & Entertainment

M&E Sales Tax Expense

Office Supplies

Outside Services

Postage and Delivery

Printing

Professional Fees - Accounting

Professional Fees - Legal

Rentals

Repairs and Maintenance

Sundry

Travel Accommodation

Travel Transportation

Vehicle Fuel

Vehicle Parking and Tolls

Vehicle Repairs and Maintenance

Suspense

Alright, let's have a closer look at these accounts.

***Asset* - Checking Account** (or Chequing account, if you prefer - just Edit the name)

This will represent your main business bank account. It is best if you can open an actual bank account just for business transactions. It is not a good idea to mix your business and personal dealings.

***Asset* - Savings Account**

It is a good idea to open another business account at the branch where your business chequing account is. This Savings account will be used for depositing a portion of your income that you will have to eventually remit to the tax agency. These include amounts for sales tax, income tax, and any government-mandated pension contributions.

Asset - PayPal or other Virtual Currency or Barter Account

Many authors make use of PayPal or similar type of service to facilitate sales or purchases, particularly when dealing with out of country (foreign currency) transactions. You will record these transactions just like you would if using your bank account. If you eventually want to convert the value in those accounts to 'cash' in your bank account then you make the transfer and record it in your books as coming out of one account and into the other.

Note - just like you should have a dedicated bank and credit card account for your business, you should also set up a dedicated PayPal account.

Asset - Petty Cash

Whether or not you keep some cash on hand for small purchases, a Petty Cash account can save you a trip to the bank. Here's an example:

You sell a paperback to your neighbour. She gives you $20.00 cash. You will record the sale, then record that you kept the cash.

Record the sale:

Account	Debit	Credit	Memo
Book Sales		20.00	Cash sale of book
Petty Cash	20.00		Cash sale of book

Keep the cash:

Account	Debit	Credit	Memo
Petty Cash		20.00	Cash withdrawal
Owner's Draw	20.00		Cash withdrawal

Asset - Accounts Receivable

This account represents money that is owed to you but hasn't yet been collected. Perhaps you gave a talk at a book fair and the organizers offered to pay your trip expenses. When you get home and have totaled your receipts you would first record them as an expense:

Account	Debit	Credit	Memo
Travel Expense	80.51		Book Fair trip costs
Sales Tax Payable	4.24		Book Fair trip costs
Petty Cash		84.75	Book Fair trip costs

Then you would send the organizer an invoice for $84.75.

Now, the nice thing about computerized accounting programs is that they provide an easy to use interface and do a lot of the background work for you. For example, you would open up the *Invoice* screen and enter the date, the customer's name, the quantity and item you provided, a description, and the cost. If you have set up your program correctly (I'll explain that later), the *Invoice* routine will calculate the (5% ?) tax ($80.51 + $4.24tx = $84.75) and make the following entries:

Account	Debit	Credit	Memo
Other Income		80.51	Book Fair trip costs
Sales Tax Payable		4.24	Book Fair trip costs
Accounts Receivable	84.75		Book Fair trip costs

When you receive the money from the customer, another routine will make the following post:

Account	Debit	Credit	Memo
Accounts Receivable		84.75	Book Fair reimbursement
Petty Cash	84.75		Book Fair reimbursement

Note - if you receive a cheque or perhaps a wire transfer, the money may end up in your bank instead of going back to petty cash. That is fine; you would just apply the $84.75 to the Bank Chequing *account instead of the* Petty Cash *account - the important thing is that you got the money.*

When both these transactions are complete the Accounts Receivable account will have a `Debit` entry of $84.75 and a `Credit` entry of $84.75 which equals $0.00 but the amounts for Travel and Sales Tax will stay on the books, which is what we want.

***Asset* - Furniture & Equipment**

This account is where you will record the cost of any office furniture or equipment you will buy for your business. You can also record the value of any equipment (like a computer) that you want to give to the business as part of your Owner's Equity (see the explanation Equity - Owner's Equity in the *It's also about organization* section).

***Asset* - Accum. Depr. Furn. & Equip.**

The abbreviation above stands for Accumulated Depreciation of Furniture and Equipment. As soon as you buy some furniture or equipment it starts to lose value. For the purposes of bookkeeping, it is generally accepted that these items depreciate at a rate of 20% per year. The good thing is that we can claim that depreciation as an expense.

Let's say you bought a new computer for $500. At the end of each year you can depreciate 20% of that $500 ($100) until the total depreciation equals the original cost. The entry would look like this:

Account	Debit	Credit	Memo
Accum.Depr.Furn.& Equip.	100.00		Annual deprec.
Depreciation Expense		100.00	Annual deprec.

Asset - Inventory

For authors, your inventory will consist of the author copies of your books that you buy from your printer, for resale. It could also include any swag items, if you're into giveaways It doesn't matter whether you pay by cheque, e-transfer from your bank, or if you pay by credit card, the entry looks pretty much the same.

In this example, let's say you bought two dozen books at your cost of $6.00 each which comes to $144.00. There was a $34.00 shipping cost, and total sales tax was $8.00. Total cost from the printer would be $186.00. The bookkeeping would look like this:

Account	Debit	Credit	Memo
Inventory	144.00		24 copies-Cookbook
Postage and Delivery	34.00		24 copies-Cookbook
Sales Tax Payable	8.00		24 copies-Cookbook
Credit Card		186.00	24 copies-Cookbook
	186.00	186.00	

So, right now, the value of your Inventory is $144.00. Hopefully, you will soon sell those, and buy more author copies.

To take this a step further, over the next eight months you bought another $576.00 worth of books from the printer. At the end of the year, your inventory account would show a value of $720.00 ($144.00 + $576.00).

Of course, one would hope that over the course of the year you have sold a batch of those, so $720.00 would not be a true value of the account. To correct this, you would do a physical count of the books on hand (maybe 38 books), calculate the cost of those books ($6 each) to get a true year-end inventory value of $228.00.

To bring the account into line, you need to make an adjustment of $492.00 (posted value of $720.00 minus on-hand value of $228.00).

The year-end adjusting entry would look like this:

Account	Debit	Credit	Memo
Inventory		492.00	Inventory adjustment
Cost Of Goods Sold	492.00		Inventory adjustment

Note - if you are adjusting the inventory of Swag (which should have its own Asset account) you would `Debit` the Advertising/Promotion account because the Cost of Goods Sold account is for items that you stock for resale, and you don't sell Swag. It is strictly for promotion.

Liability **- Credit Card**

We use our credit cards much like we use our bank accounts, and the entries are very similar; purchases create a `Credit` to either the bank account or credit card, and when money is added to the account that is a `Debit`. The difference is that credit card purchases are actually loans from the credit card company, and loans are liabilities because they have to be paid back.

Note - it is recommended that you have a credit card dedicated to business purchases only. Look for one that gives you rebates on purchases, and has no annual fee.

Liability **- Owed to Owner**

The Owed to Owner account is where we put amounts for purchases paid for with your personal (out of pocket) funds. Let's say you are at a book fair and there is an author selling a book on copywriting, which you purchase with cash from your pocket ($20.00). The entry would be as follows:

Account	Debit	Credit	Memo
Owed to Owner		20.00	Bought copywriting book
Education	20.00		Bought copywriting book

Sometimes, the opposite happens. You might go to the grocery store and buy laundry detergent ($15.95) which you accidently pay for with your business credit card. Since laundry detergent is not an eligible business expense, you would owe the business $15.95. The entry looks like this:

Account	Debit	Credit	Memo
Owed to Owner	15.95		Personal purchase
Credit Card		15.95	Personal purchase

Let's take this a step further. At the end of the month, you decide to settle the Owed to Owner account. A report of the account would look something like this:

Owed to Owner as of November 30, 2020

Date	Memo	Debit	Credit
11-06-2020	Bought copywriting book		20.00
11-23-2020	Personal purchase	15.95	
	Balance		4.05

So, there is a balance on the account of $4.05. Does this mean you owe the business bank account $4.05, or does the business bank account owe you $4.05?

First of all, keep in mind that we want to bring the Owed to Owner account to $0.00. Since it has a Credit balance of $4.05, we now need to Debit the account by $4.05. If we are going to `Debit` the Owed to Owner account, then we will have to `Credit` the business bank account. The entry looks like this:

Account	Debit	Credit	Memo
Owed to Owner	4.05		To clear account
Bank Chequing		4.05	To clear account

Remember that rule of thumb you learned in the *It's all about the money* section (Deposits = Debits). Since the bank account is being credited, then money is coming out, which means the business owes the owner (you) $4.05. Write yourself a cheque.

To finish this off, let's update that report for the Owed to Owner account:

Owed to Owner as of November 30, 2020

Date	Memo	Debit	Credit
11-06-2020	Bought copywriting book		20.00
11-23-2020	Personal purchase	15.95	
11-30-2020	To clear account	4.05	.
	Balance	0.00	0.00

Liability - Sales Tax Payable

Depending on where you live, sales tax will likely have an abbreviation. In my region we have a Provincial Sales Tax of 8% (PST), a Goods and Services Tax of 5% (GST), and Harmonized Sales Tax of 13% (HST). Thankfully, they are not all applied at the same time. My point, however, is that the Sales Tax Payable account may be called the HST Payable account, or the VAT Payable account, or whatever abbreviation your regional tax agency uses, so be prepared to be flexible with this name. Also be prepared to see a Sales Tax Payable account for each kind of tax in your region.

Anyway, if a transaction has sales tax, whether you are selling a book or editing service or purchasing something for your business, this is the account where the tax amount is recorded. When you buy something, the sales tax is a `Debit` to the account. When you sell something the sales tax is a `Credit` to the account.

Note - because you record the sales tax in any transaction, separately, it is important when recording that sale or purchase that only the cost of the item or service (before tax) is recorded in the Income and Expense accounts. There is an example, further on, in the explanation of 'Liability - Accounts Payable'.

Now, according to my tax agency (yours may differ) if a business has less than $30,000 in annual income it is not required to charge and subsequently remit sales tax. Some of you with low sales (under $30,000 / year) may be tempted to go this route but I advise against it. The reason is that if you elect to charge sales tax on your products, you can also claim any sales tax on products that you buy. This is especially advantageous in the first year or two when your purchases may exceed your sales. If you paid out more sales tax than you brought in, then the tax agency will owe YOU money. When you start a business, money will probably be tight for a while, so it's nice to get something back. Your tax agency website will have information on setting up your business for this.

For more on this, see the section *Sales Taxes - Recording, Calculating, Filing.*

Liability **- Accounts Payable**

This account represents money that you owe your vendors but haven't yet paid. Perhaps you had a graphic artist do some design work for a book cover and she's sent you an invoice for $250.00. Now, the nice thing about computerized accounting programs is that they provide an easy to use interface, and do a lot of the background work for you.

For example, you would open up the *Bills* screen and enter the date, the vendor's name, the quantity and item provided, and the cost. If you have set up your program correctly (I'll explain that later), the *Bills* routine will calculate the (5% ?) tax ($250.00 + $12.50tx = $262.50) and make the following entries:

Account	Debit	Credit	Memo
Outside Services	250.00		Cover art
Sales Tax Payable	12.50		Cover art
Accounts Payable		262.50	Cover art

When you pay the vendor, another routine will make the following post:

Account	Debit	Credit	Memo
Accounts Payable	262.50		Cover art payment
Bank Account		262.50	Cover art payment

When both these transactions are complete the Accounts Payable account will have a `Credit` entry of $262.50 and a `Debit` entry of $262.50 which equals $0.00.

***Equity* - Opening Balances**

It is common for authors to engage in business activities before the opening day of their bookkeeping. So, one of the first things to record is the state of your business as of the first day of your bookkeeping.

You will list Assets like the bank balance, estimated current value of your equipment, etc.; Liabilities which could be funds loaned to you for your business, or credit card amounts for anything purchased for your business prior to opening day; Equity such as money you invested; and Expenses like the value of any office supplies. The sum of these amounts will be considered your Opening Balance which is essentially what your business is worth on day one.

Note - Your Opening Balance entries will be dated as of the last day of the fiscal year previous to your first fiscal year of bookkeeping. This is so you will have an accurate record of transactions that happened only during the fiscal year, itself. In other words, if you started tracking your finances in 2020, and your fiscal year is January 1st to December 31st, then your Opening Balance entries would be dated for December 31st 2019.

Equity - Retained Earnings

At the end of each fiscal year the Income accounts and the Expense accounts get emptied (automatically by the software) into the Retained Earnings account. If you had more income than you had expenses, then you should show a profit for the year. If the total of your expenses is greater than the total of your income, then you will show a loss for the year. The balance in the Retained Earnings account will increase or decrease from year to year but is cumulative from the start date of your bookkeeping.

Equity - Owner's Equity

Amounts posted to this account represent any personal funds that you have invested in the business, or the value of any equipment or property that you personally are donating to the business. For examples, take a look at the *Equity* - Owner's Equity explanation in the *It's also about organization* section.

Equity - Owner's Draw

As a Sole Proprietor, you will not get a paycheque. If you want to be paid then you must draw money from the company. As the owner, it is up to you how much you take, and how often you do this. For examples, take a look at the Equity - Owner's Draw explanation in the *It's also about organization* section.

Income - Book Royalties

When a distributor sells a digital or print version of your book, they send you your cut which is known as a royalty. The amounts you `Debit` to your bank account get recorded in this account as a `Credit`.

Income - Book Sales

When you sell directly to the reader, perhaps at a book fair or from your own website, as with the royalties, the amount (before tax) from the sale is recorded in this income account.

Income - Interest Income

Perhaps you have a bank account that pays you interest if you keep a certain balance. This is where you record the interest the bank pays you.

Income - Other Income

There are a number of ways, other than writing books, that an author can generate income. If those avenues are a regular activity then you may want to create a dedicated Income account. Otherwise, for those rare occasions where you are paid for a book talk or some editing service, you can record that income into this miscellaneous account.

Income - Reimbursed Expenses

Perhaps you travelled to give a talk, and in doing so had to pay for a train ticket, hotel stay, meals, cab fare, etc. You would record those payments in the appropriate expense accounts. However, if the organizer of the event offers to cover those costs (once you send her the receipts) when you get the money back, this is where you record the amount.

Note - the reimbursement doesn't have to equal the expense; that will depend on the arrangement you make with the organizer.

Expense - Advertising & Promotion

There are many way you can promote your work, and all those costs can go into this account - or you can make individual accounts for things like Displays, Website, Amazon Ads, etc.

Expense - Bank / Credit Card Charges

Use this account to record bank and credit card FEES as opposed to INTEREST which is recorded in a separate account (Bank / Credit Card Interest).

Expense - Bank / Credit Card Interest

This is the account to which you post all those pesky interest charges the banks and credit card companies like to ding you with.

Expense - Cost of Goods Sold

This account is where you post any costs incurred in the manufacture of your physical product. Since your physical product is a book, you would record the cost of each book that you have sold in the Cost of Goods Sold account. For our purposes, this is an entry you can do at year-end, as an inventory adjustment (See the explanation in the Asset - Inventory section above).

Expense - Depreciation

Depreciation is the reduction of an object's value due to age. This is something you will calculate at the end of each fiscal year by determining the original cost of your item, and dividing that amount by the number of years that you think its useful life will be. Office equipment is generally considered to have a five year life-span. So, for a computer that cost $1,000.00, at the end of the fiscal year, for the next five years, you can depreciate it by $200.00.

To record the depreciation, there will be two accounts involved:

1) The Asset account Accumulated Depreciation of Furniture and Equipment which is often abbreviated to Accum. Depr. Furn. & Equip.

2) The Expense account Depreciation.

The journal entry would look like this:

Account	Debit	Credit	Memo
Accum.Depr.Furn.& Equip.		200.00	F&E Depreciation
Depreciation	200.00		F&E Depreciation

Note - keeping in mind that you may buy furniture or equipment at staggered intervals, you can keep the adjustment simple by just taking 20% of the difference between the balance of the Furniture & Equipment account and the Accum. Depr. Furn. & Equip. account. At least until the difference is less than $200 then you may as well depreciate the balance.

You'll know you have depreciated all of your Furniture and Equipment account when its balance equals the amount in the Accum. Depr. Furn. & Equip. account.

Expense **- Donations**

It is not uncommon for an author to donate a book (or several) to a fund-raising event. While it is a magnanimous gesture, it can be hard to claim that as an expense to lower your taxable income. Instead, I recommend that any product or service you wish to donate be posted as an Advertising / Promotion expense. Many tax agencies prefer that donations be monetary so there is no question as to the actual value of the donation. If you do make a donation of any sort, make sure that you get an official receipt from the registered charity for the monetary value if you wish to claim it.

Expense - Dues and Subscriptions

Any amounts you pay for memberships or subscriptions to print or digital media, that is business-related, gets posted here. Many software programs, for example, have an option where you can either buy the software outright, or pay a monthly subscription. That monthly subscription would be posted here. See the example below:

Account	Debit	Credit	Memo
Dues & Subscriptions	49.95		Software
Credit Card		49.95	Software

Expense - Education / Workshops

If you take any writing courses, or workshops, you can post those registration costs here.

Expense - Equipment Rental

Maybe you lease your computer equipment, or perhaps you rented a booth at a book fair, or a sound system for a book launch. Post those costs here.

Expense - Exchange Gain or Loss

This account is for recording the apparent difference in amounts when a transfer is made between two accounts with different currencies. For more information, see the explanation of *Transfers* in the *Bookkeeping Procedures* section.

Expense - Interest - Ineligible

If you are late remitting any sort of government payment, they will hit you with an interest charge (sometimes called a finance charge). Unlike bank and credit card interest charges, any interest charged by the government is not an eligible (claimable) expense. This also applies to municipalities who may charge interest on late payments for property tax or water bills, etc.

Expense - Internet Expense

If you have a dedicated office internet connection, *just for your business*, then you can post those charges here. If you have a home office that shares the Internet connection with the household you will need to keep track of the charges in a spreadsheet, throughout the fiscal year, then calculate how much you used the Internet for your writing. That portion (say 50%) will then be part of your Home Office expenses that your accountant will record and file on a separate tax form. See the section on *Home Office Expenses* for more detail on this.

Expense - Licenses and Permits

This account is where you would record costs for a business licence, or perhaps you are having a book launch and need a special permit for fireworks or a liquor licence.

Expense - Meals & Entertainment

You are allowed to claim a portion of meals (and/or drinks) purchased while conducting your business. I would check with your tax agency to learn the eligibility rules for your region, but generally, if you are away from home for more than twelve hours, or you take your editor / publisher / local bookstore owner, etc. to lunch then you can claim 50% of the cost of the meal. The tricky part is keeping track of this because, at the time, you will pay 100% of the bill.

Here's an example: You meet with your graphic artist at a coffee shop to discuss a new book cover. You both have the soup and sandwich special. You pick up the tab which is $24.00 + tax (say, $2.40). When you get home, you would make the following entry:

Account	Debit	Credit	Memo
Meals & Entertainment	24.00		Lunch with designer
M&E Sales Tax Expense	1.20		Lunch with designer
Sales Tax Payable	1.20		Lunch with designer
Credit Card		26.40	Lunch with designer

You will notice that the sales tax of $2.40 was split between two accounts, each with $1.20. In order to reconcile our Credit Card account, we need to show the whole cost, however, because the tax agency will only allow you to claim 50% it is important to divide the sales tax now so we don't have to dig through all our entries at the end of the year to make an adjustment.

Now, although you are only allowed to use 50% of the sales tax on meals to reduce your sales tax payable (remember, sales tax payable is the sales tax you collected from selling books minus the sales tax you paid from buying stuff), the nice thing is that you can claim the other 50% of the meals sales tax as a straight expense. This is why we have the M&E Sales Tax Expense account.

The important thing, here, is that you let your accountant know, at year-end, how you have calculated this.

Expense - M&E Sales Tax Expense

As discussed above, the purpose of this account is to collect the 50% of the meals sales tax that isn't eligible to reduce your overall sales tax payable. Again, it can still be claimed as a straight-up expense.

***Expense* - Office Supplies**

Pens, pencils, printer paper, thumb drives, stamps, envelopes, boxes, etc. can all be posted to this account.

***Expense* - Outside Services**

Sometime called subcontractors, these are the people/companies that you get to help you (ie) editors, graphic designers, even musicians if you hire them for a book launch.

***Expense* - Postage and Delivery**

If you receive or send anything out by mail or courier, the costs can be posted to this account. Sometimes, if a package crosses an international border, you may have to pay brokerage (not to be confused with sales tax that is sometimes tacked on by customs). It's up to you whether you create an expense account for brokerage, or just lump it in with the delivery charges.

***Expense* - Printing**

Do not use this account to record the cost of print runs for your books (those costs are recorded in the Inventory account). This account is for printing costs of flyers, business cards, posters, etc. that you have made by a print shop.

***Expense* - Professional Fees - Accounting**

This is where you record the fees you pay to your accountant and/or bookkeeper. Even though this guide will give you a good start, if you get stuck it's not a bad idea to have a freelance bookkeeper help you to get set-up. Kijiji is a good place to find one.

Expense - Professional Fees - Legal

If you deal with contracts, particularly if you have an agent or are considering a joint project with another writer, it's a good idea to have a lawyer check over any agreements. This account is where those fees are posted.

Expense - Repairs and Maintenance

Things occasionally need fixing, or just a little TLC like a squeaky file drawer that could use a squirt of WD40. The cost of anything you need to buy to keep your work environment running smoothly gets posted to this account.

Expense - Sundry

This is sort of a miscellaneous account where you would post any small amounts that don't easily slot into another category. Perhaps you bought some flowers to brighten up your display at a book fair. You could post that to Advertising and Promotion, or put it in Sundry. Just don't get lazy and use this account too often - it's one of those accounts that can make a tax auditor raise an eyebrow.

Expense - Travel Accommodation

Let's say one of your books has been picked up for a movie version, and you have to go to Hollywood. Your hotel costs would be posted here.

Expense - Travel Transportation

Of course, if you're going to oversee the casting of your lead character for the big screen version of your blockbuster, then you'll have to get there (go ahead, fly first class). Any costs for planes, trains, and automobiles, even if it's just an Uber or a subway ride, get posted here.

Expense - Vehicle Fuel

In the *Home Office Expenses* section we looked at how Sole Proprietors can claim a portion of home expenses as a business expense. Included in that is a provision for automobile expenses. If you are using your own vehicle, then any gas you buy will be calculated along with the other Home Office Expenses.

However; if you rent a vehicle while in Hollywood, or rent a van to pick up a large print run of books, then the fuel you would use for that trip can be posted here as a straight business expense.

If you are incorporated, then fuel that goes into the vehicle you have listed under the Company name can be recorded here.

Expense - Vehicle Parking and Tolls

All parking and toll road fees can always be claimed as a business expense - don't lose those little slips!

Expense - Vehicle Repairs and Maintenance

In the *Home Office Expenses* section, under the provision for automobile expenses, should be a calculation for vehicle repair or maintenance bills. You can claim the percentage as defined by your mileage log.

If you are incorporated, then any bills for oil changes, or repairs, etc. for the vehicle you have listed under the Company name can be recorded here.

Expense - Suspense

I always like to have a Suspense account. It comes in very handy as a temporary holding account when I don't have enough information to decide which specific account an amount should be posted to. Perhaps you are reconciling your bank and notice there's a deposit there you don't recognize. Was it income from a book sale? Did someone send you a refund? Is it an error by the bank? Until you know what this deposit is for you can temporarily post it to the Suspense account, as follows:

Account	Debit	Credit	Memo
Bank Chequing	75.00		Unknown deposit
Suspense		75.00	Unknown deposit

So, later on, you find out the print shop that screwed up your posters has sent you a refund. Depending on your accounting software, you may be able to open up the posting above and change the Suspense account to the Printing account. Or you can do a journal entry, as follows:

Account	Debit	Credit	Memo
Suspense	75.00		To reallocate deposit
Printing		75.00	To reallocate deposit

Note - you should always find a permanent home for any amounts in the Suspense account. Do not close out a fiscal year without doing so.

So, while these accounts will give you a good start, remember that you can always customize your list, to some degree, to suit your specific needs.

BOOKKEEPING PROCEDURES

Now that you have some insight into the main function and basic terminology of bookkeeping, we will look at the essential tasks you should do daily (more or less), monthly, and annually to keep your books current and accurate. Before setting up your software program it is good to know how bookkeeping tasks are integrated, and the reason for doing them. The following overview of these procedures will also help you to understand what your program is doing behind the scenes.

DAILY STUFF

Essentially, the daily stuff includes the everyday-type transactions that occur in the course of running your writing business. Mainly, you sell your work and you buy supplies. How frequently you buy or sell stuff will determine how often you actually need to post these transactions in your books. You don't necessarily have to enter everything on the day it happens, but make sure you obtain a paper copy of any transaction (something a tax auditor may ask to see) and don't leave these copies sitting in your "To Be Posted" folder for longer than a week. If you're not generating many transactions, perhaps schedule a certain time each week to catch up on all your entries.

Invoices and Sale Receipts

We use the terms *Invoice* and *Sales Receipt* when selling our product to a customer. The difference between the two is whether the customer pays you the moment you hand over the signed copy of your book or if they pay you sometime later.

An *Invoice* is used when you have provided a product or service and don't expect to be paid immediately. You will create a customer account and assign the invoice to that account. This creates a *Receivable*. In your Chart of Accounts you will see there is an Accounts Receivable account. This is where your software will automatically post any invoice amounts (as a `Debit`) that you issue to customers. When you receive payment, you will apply the payment to the invoice and the program will automatically `Credit` the amount to the Accounts Receivable account. A report of the Accounts Receivable account will let you see how much money is currently owed to you at any particular time.

A *Sales Receipt* is used when you receive payment immediately on providing the product or service. An example would be selling your books at a book fair. A reader comes to your booth and buys a signed copy of your latest Space Opera. You hand them the book and they hand you $20. To enter a Sales Receipt it isn't always necessary to create an individual customer file. If you already have one because they are a frequent buyer, then fine, otherwise you can just create a Miscellaneous Customer file to use for individual sales, or if the book fair was really busy and you had lots of sales you may want to create a customer file called Book Fair August 15 2020 and post the total amount you received on that day as one entry. This type of transaction does not create a *Receivable* because you got the money right away and nothing is owed to you.

Vendor Bills and Purchase Receipts

A *Vendor Bill* is something you get when you have received a product or service but have not yet paid for it. Perhaps you have delayed payment terms with your editor who has proofed your manuscript and sent you a bill for $225. This creates a *Payable*. In your Chart of Accounts you will see there is an Accounts Payable account. This is where the software will automatically post any amounts (as a `Credit`) that you apply to your vendor files. When you make the payment, you will apply it to the *Vendor Bill* and the program will automatically `Debit` the amount to the Accounts Payable account. A report of the Accounts Payable account will let you see how much money you owe to vendors at any particular time.

Like a *Sales Receipt*, a *Purchase Receipt* is used when you pay for something the moment you receive it. A good example is buying a ream of printer paper at the office supply store. It doesn't matter if you hand over cash, use your bank card, or pay with your credit card. As far as the store is concerned, you have received the product and they have received payment so they issue a *Purchase Receipt*. This type of transaction does not get recorded in the Accounts Payable account because the product has been paid for and there is no debt.

Hey, wait a minute! If you used your credit card, then wouldn't you owe a debt to the credit card provider? Well, yes, you would. If you go back and take a quick look in the *Chart of Accounts* section, you will see the Accounts Payable and Credit Card accounts are both Liability accounts. Anything recorded in those Liability accounts represents an amount you owe. The difference is that the Accounts Payable account represents amounts you owe directly to suppliers. A Credit Card account, however, is more like a loan from a third party. You still owe the credit card company but those amounts are kept separate.

Transfers

You will likely do a few transfers during a month, moving amounts from one money account to another. You may transfer funds from your bank account to pay the balance on your credit card account. Or you may transfer money from your PayPal account into your Bank account.

Authors often have to deal with foreign currencies, though this doesn't have to be too complicated. Here's a simple example using a US$ PayPal account and a Canadian $ Bank account:

I have $400 USD in my PayPal account that I want to transfer to my CDN Bank.

The currency exchange rate for the transfer is 1.25

$400 USD x 1.25 = $500 CDN

In the real world, $400 comes out of PayPal, and $500 ends up in my Bank.

However, when you record this in your bookkeeping, those two amounts aren't equal so you have to record the difference in an Exchange Gain or Loss Expense account. The Journal Entry would look like this:

Account	Debit	Credit	Memo
Bank Chequing	495.00		Transfer
Bank Charges	5.00		Transfer Fee
PayPal Account		400.00	Transfer
Exchange Gain or Loss		100.00	Transfer
	500.00	500.00	

You will notice that, just for fun, I included a bank charge for the transfer to show the amount that really ended up in your bank was $495.00.

MONTHLY BOOKKEEPING TASKS

A few days after a month has ended, it is a good idea to run some monthly financial reports to see how things are going. Before you do so, however, you will need to make sure your bookkeeping is up to date. Here are the tasks that need to be completed before running your month-end reports:

Record your home office expenses - although you will enter your home office expenses in a spreadsheet, rather than your bookkeeping software, it is a good idea to record them in the month they occur. See the section *Home Office Expenses* for more information on this.

Make sure that you have issued *Invoices* or *Sales Receipts* for all sales made during the month.

Make sure that you have posted all payments received during the month.

Make sure you have deposited all payments received during the month.

Make sure that you have posted all *Vendor Bills* and *Purchase Receipts.*

Make sure you have posted all payments to vendors during the month.

Reconcile your business credit card statement.

Reconcile your business bank statement.

Note 1 - when reconciling your statements you will notice any transactions that you may have forgotten, missed, or were unaware of. It is also good way to see if everything has been recorded properly - and even banks make mistakes.

Note 2 - sometimes the bank or credit card company will issue statements that don't line up with the beginning and end of a month. If that's the case, you may have to put off doing your 'month-end' until you get the statement that covers the end of the month you want to close. The reason for this is that it might be time to file your Sales Tax with the tax agency, and you want to make sure you have recorded all the applicable Sales Tax for that particular period even though time might be a little tight between when you actually get all the info you need, and the date you need to file.

Note 3 - many authors use PayPal or some other virtual coin or bartering hub. Set these up in your books like you would set up a bank account, and reconcile them accordingly.

Okay, now that we have everything recorded for the month, it is time to run some reports.

Note- like everything else mentioned in this section, I will show you how to run reports in the software sections.

Trial Balance

A *Trial Balance* report shows the monetary value in each active account, at a certain date. Some of the amounts will be in the `Debit` column and some will be in the `Credit` column. As mentioned in the section *It's also about organization*, the type of account usually determines whether the balance will show on the `Debit` side or the `Credit` side. Here's a review:

```
Asset accounts       Debit
Liability accounts   Credit
Equity accounts      Credit
Income accounts      Credit
Expense accounts     Debit
```

When you have run this report you will notice that on the bottom line the `Debits` will always equal the `Credits`.

Income Statement / Profit and Loss Report

The *Income Statement,* which is alternatively called a *Profit and Loss Report*, lists only the *Income* and *Expense* accounts. It shows how much money has gone out of the business during the period (Expenses), and how much money you have taken in (Income).

Keeping in mind we are using accrual-based accounting (see the section titled *Bookkeeping Procedures*), sometimes this includes amounts that have not yet gone into or out of your bank account. Included in this report are sales you may have invoiced for but haven't yet received funds, or expenses from vendor bills that you have entered but not yet paid.

The bottom line of this report will say *Net Income* or *Profit/Loss*, and will either be a positive number because you made a profit that period, or a negative number because your expenses that period were greater than your income. However, don't be discouraged if a period shows a loss as can happen from time to time, especially if you'd just ordered a load of books. Hopefully, when you get to December 31st. and run the report for the whole year, you will see a positive number on the bottom line.

Balance Sheet

Whereas the *Income Statement* lists only the Income and Expense accounts, the *Balance Sheet* only lists the Asset, Liability, and Equity accounts. And just like the income minus the expenses gives you the profit (or loss); Assets minus Liabilities = Equity.

The top section of the *Balance Sheet* lists your Assets, such as the balance of your bank accounts, any money owed to you in the Accounts Receivable account, and the current value of your equipment.

The middle section of the *Balance Sheet* lists your Liabilities, such as money that you owe vendors in the Accounts Payable account, the current balance owing on your credit card, the outstanding balance on any loans you have taken out.

The bottom section of the *Balance Sheet* lists your Equity. It will show the money you have pumped into the business (Owner's Equity), the money you have taken out of the business (Owner's Draw), and the Retained Earnings.

Ideally, the *Total Equity* should be a positive number to show your company has some worth, but don't worry too much if it initially shows a negative amount. Many businesses start off in the hole.

Accounts Receivable Report

This report lists any invoices that you have issued for which you have not received payment. The total of this report should equal the amount shown in the Accounts Receivable account in the *Trial Balance* for the same period. If you have any invoices that have been outstanding for more than a month, send the customer a statement with a polite but firm request for payment.

Accounts Payable Report

This report lists any vendor bills that you have received but have not yet paid. The total of this report should equal the amount shown in the Accounts Payable account in the *Trial Balance* for the same period. Unless you have delayed payment terms, or an agreement with a supplier, avoid letting bills go past 30 days without payment. Interest charges may be applied, and those can eat away at your hard-earned profits.

Sales Tax Payable Report

You can see at a glance how much is currently in the Sales Tax Payable account by finding that line in the *Trial Balance*. Depending on the month you may have to run this report in order to make your sales tax filing with your tax agency. For more information on this refer to the section titled *Sales Taxes - Recording, Calculating, Filing*.

Put some cash aside

No, this is not a report. It is something you should do at the end of each month to cover any sales tax or income tax that you will eventually have to pay to your tax agency. It is a good idea to talk to your accountant to figure out how much to set aside. Personally, I always keep aside enough to cover any amount shown in the Sales Tax Payable account in the *Trial Balance*. Plus, I set aside 25% of my *Net Income* (15% for income tax and 10% for required government pension contribution) as found on the *Income Statement*. I have a dedicated savings account that I transfer these funds into, and you should have one, too.

I also find this is a good time to pay any balance on my credit card. In fact, I try to pay my credit card balance every couple of weeks. Credit card companies make a lot of interest from account balances that go just one day past the payment due date. Don't let them pick your pocket. Often there is less than two weeks between the date you receive your statement, and the date that payment is due. For this reason, I regularly check (and pay) my credit card accounts, online.

FISCAL YEAR END TASKS

The Fiscal Year End, which for you Sole Proprietors will always be December 31st, is when you get the clearest picture on how profitable your year has been. You'll be able to look back and identify your big expenditures, and which products were most profitable. Pretty well every business has fluctuations, periods when sales and expenses are higher or lower, so having done a full-year cycle you can now see when those periods are, and perhaps adjust your purchasing or advertising strategy accordingly.

Just like you did for the Month-End, you will now run all the same reports except this time you specify the period as the whole year (ie) January 01 2020 to December 31, 2020. Once you have done this, look them over very carefully. There are some things that you may want to clean up. Here are a few suggestions:

Accounts Receivable and Accounts Payable

As part of your month-end procedures, you likely followed up on any amounts that are in these accounts (as above), but if not you should do so now.

Write-off bad debts

If you have outstanding receivables; invoices that customers have not paid from several months ago despite your best efforts to get them to pay, you may want to classify them as a Bad Debt. When doing so, you will date the Journal Entry for the last day of the Fiscal Year you are closing. For more information on this see the segment Bad Debt / Write-Offs in the *Common Terms* section.

Owed To Owner / Owner's Draw / Owner's Equity

The Owed to Owner account represents 'out-of-pocket' amounts for business purchases you made with your personal cash. Of course, that can go the other way, like if you bought a bag of cat kibble and used the business bank or credit card. Yes, I know cats make great paperweights and should be considered a legitimate business expense, but the tax agency won't agree.

If the Owed to Owner amount is on the `Credit` side, then the business owes you. I suggest you clean out this account by issuing a business cheque to yourself (`Debit` Owed To Owner / `Credit` the Bank Chequing account), or by making a journal entry to transfer the amount to the Owner's Equity account, as below:

Account	Debit	Credit	Memo
Owed To Owner	108.65		To clear account
Owner's Equity		108.65	To clear account

If the Owed to Owner amount is on the `Debit` side, then you owe the business. I suggest you either make a deposit to your business bank account (`Credit` Owed to Owner / `Debit` the Bank Chequing account) or make a journal entry to transfer the amount to the Owner's Draw account, as below:

Account	Debit	Credit	Memo
Owed To Owner		58.75	To clear account
Owner's Draw	55.75		To clear account

Do an inventory count and adjustment

Throughout the year you will likely have bought some author copies of your books, and sold them. At the time you received each batch, you will have recorded the transaction with a `Debit` to your Inventory account by the value of the books (your cost before taxes), and a `Credit` to your Bank Chequing or Credit Card account.

At the end of the year, you will physically count all of the books you have on hand and calculate the value of your inventory. Now that you know the value of your inventory at the beginning of the year, and the value of your inventory at the end of the year, you need to make an adjusting entry. Here's an example:

Perhaps this was your first year as an author and you hadn't yet published a book, therefore you didn't have any to sell. Your inventory count of books on hand would be $0.00. However, congratulations and break out the bubbly, your debut novel *Mister Fry's First Murder* hits the market and you order your first batch of author copies. Let's say you bought two dozen books at your cost of $6.00 each which comes to $144.00.

So, right now, the value of your Inventory account is $144.00. Hopefully, you will sell those, and buy more author copies. Over the next eight months you buy another $576.00 worth of books from the printer. At the end of the year, your Inventory account would show a value of $720.00 ($144.00 + $576.00). Of course, one would hope that over the course of the year you have sold a batch of those, so $720.00 would not be a true value of the account.

To correct this, do a physical count of the books on hand (now 38 books), calculate the cost of those books ($6 each) to get a true year-end inventory value of $228.00. To bring the account into line, make an adjustment of $492.00 (posted value of $720.00 minus on-hand value of $228.00).

The year-end adjusting entry would look like this:

Account	Debit	Credit	Memo
Inventory		492.00	Year-end adjustment
Cost Of Goods Sold	492.00		Year-end adjustment

Since the Cost Of Goods Sold is an expense account, you are recognizing that there is cost to produce the books you sell (a sale is not all profit), and this expense will help to lower your taxable income that you file with the tax agency.

Suspense

Yes, suspense in our books is usually a good thing, but not here. The Suspense account is where you apply any amounts that you are unsure as to where they belong. This is a temporary measure, perhaps so you can reconcile a bank account. But sooner or later you have to find a proper home for these amounts and Year-End is definitely that time. Make a decision and use a journal entry to move the amount(s) out of the Suspense account.

Home Expense Report

If you haven't already, now is the time to dig out all those utility, insurance, property tax, fuel, and repair bills and receipts you'd stuffed in a drawer, or in the glove box of your Maserati, and total them up in a spreadsheet. See the section: *Home Office Expenses* for more information on this.

Send a set of financial reports to your accountant

Here is a list of reports to give your accountant at the end of the year:

Trial Balance - as of December 31st of the year just ended.

Income Statement - for the period January 1st to December 31st of the year just ended.

Balance Sheet - as of December 31st of the year just ended.

The accountant may also ask for activity reports of individual accounts. Those you can send when they are requested.

Many accountants will also ask for a backup file of your accounting software, particularly if you use QuickBooks. This can really expedite their work, and by extension save you some money in accounting fees.

Now that you have reached the end of this section, you should have a basic understanding of bookkeeping as it pertains to the writing profession.

The next two sections will deal with the bookkeeping software programs I have selected to help you to create and maintain your own set of books.

USING SOFTWARE

The next two sections are dedicated to getting GnuCash and QuickBooks set up to handle the needs of an author. I will also provide some examples of the common tasks you will do to keep your bookkeeping up to date.

I selected GnuCash as the free option because it seemed to have the simplest interface yet still have the functionality needed.

I selected QuickBooks as the software to purchase (or subscribe to) because, frankly, I love it.

However, there are lots of other accounting programs to choose from, and you may prefer, or may already use, something else. That is totally fine. If you're comfortable with what you have you may want to just skim the next two sections to see if there is anything you might want to adapt to your particular package.

Please note that the purpose of the following sections is to help you configure and start working with the software in a manner suited to authors. It is not intended to be a complete tutorial on the program's capabilities. There are plenty of tutorial links provided within the software under 'Help'. There are also many YouTube videos. If you are still undecided on whether to go with GnuCash or QuickBooks, perhaps view a few of the video tutorials for each to get an idea of the interface.

If at anytime you feel you need more instruction or advice than is found in this book, a simple search of your question on the Internet will yield a myriad of answers.

GNUCASH

I made GnuCash the free software choice because it seems to be one of the simplest and less cumbersome packages that is not beholden to *the cloud.* I prefer to have important stuff readily accessible at all times on my own computer. GnuCash may not have the prettiest interface or lots of bells and whistles but it's quite functional and, for those who haven't yet achieved best-seller status, the price is right. Having said that, it never hurts to donate a few dollars to the developer. I have nothing to do with the company but, as an author, I know what it is like to survive on the generosity of others.

Naturally, if you do not wish to use GnuCash, you can skip this section.

INSTALLING AND CONFIGURING GNUCASH

I suggest that you first create a GnuCash directory in your computer's file directory, and select it to store the files. Then you can download the program file from www.gnucash.org

When installing, select the option for a Desktop icon.

Once the program is installed click on the Desktop icon to open it up.

Click **File** (top left of the screen) and select **New File** - it will open a setup window.

New Account Hierarchy Setup will be highlighted - click **[Next]**.

New Book Options will be highlighted - just click **[Next].**

Choose Currency will be highlighted - your country's currency should show in the currency box - if it shows an incorrect currency, click on the arrow to drop down the currency menu and choose yours - then click **[Next]**.

Before we go further, we should enter your company information so that it will appear on reports and invoices:

Click **File** on the top menu, then **Properties**.

When the window opens click the **[Business]** tab.

Type in your Company Name, either your business name (Peter Pan Stories Inc.) or your own name if that is what you operate under.

Type in your Mailing Address, and fill in any other fields as you may want to appear on an invoice.

Go to the **[Counters]** tab and change the "0" in the *Invoice Numbers* box to "1".

In the **[Tax]** tab, enter your tax ID # - this is the number you put on forms when filing your taxes.

Click **[OK]** to save everything and exit.

Click **[Finish]**.

Click **[Apply]**.

At this point you have to give your bookkeeping file a name (ie) *Author Financial Books*, or *Peter Pan Stories Inc.* - the data format (top box) should be **xml**.

This screen also allows you to choose the directory on your computer where the file will reside - the default is your desktop but select the GnuCash directory you created earlier. When you click **[Save As]** the window will close and you will have an icon on your desktop to open your bookkeeping file.

Okay, on the top menu bar, click on **Edit** then **Preferences** then **Accounting Period**.

This is where you will select the start and end dates of your Fiscal Year. Most of you will be self-employed so your fiscal year is the same as the calendar year (ie) 01/01/2020 - 12/31/2020.

We'll keep the Relative selection.

The Accounts section is where you can select your local currency if it is not already the default.

In the **[Business]** tab you should activate the box for Enable Extra Buttons.

Adjust the items in the Date/Time window as you see fit.

In the General area you can change the frequency that the program automatically saves the company file. I would set it somewhere between 5 minutes and 30 minutes.

The only other place you may need to make a preference change is the Reports section - does it show the current currency?

Click **[Close]** when you have finished with the Preferences window.

SETTING UP THE CHART OF ACCOUNTS

Right, let's turn our attention to the main ACCOUNTS window. This is the window you will always see when you first open GnuCash.

You should see a list of your main account categories, as such:

>Assets

>Equity

>Expenses

>Income

>Liabilities

Click each of the little arrows to expose all the sub-accounts.

This listing is the Chart of Accounts.

There are accounts here that we won't need and can delete, and other accounts that we'll need to add. This next section will take a little while to work through but do all of the steps described to set up your Chart of Accounts properly. A bit of time spent now will save you a lot of time, later.

To delete an account, (ie) **Dining** highlight the account and hit the **[Delete]** icon in the top menu bar - go ahead, there's another expense account called **Meals** under **Travel** that we can use instead.

To add an account, first highlight the main category in your Chart of Accounts - in this case **Assets**, click the **[New]** icon - go ahead and type *Inventory* in the Account *Name* box.

Hit your Tab key to get down into the Description box and type *Inventory on hand* then Tab once more.

Click the **[OK]** button to add the account to your list.

Let's add a couple more **Asset** accounts:

Click the **[New]** icon then type *Equipment* in the Account Name and Description boxes - then tab and click **[OK]**.

Now highlight the **Equipment** account because we're going to make a couple of sub-accounts:

Click the **[New]** icon then type *Equipment Purchased* in the Account Name and Description boxes - then tab and click **[OK]**.

Click the **[New]** icon then type *Accum. Depr. Equip.* in the Account Name and Description boxes - then tab and click OK.

Now we'll add some **Expense** accounts:

Highlight **Expenses**, then click the **[New]** button.

Type *Bank / Credit Card Interest* in the Account Name and Description boxes - then Tab and click **[OK]**.

Ready for the next one?

Highlight **Expenses**, then click the **[New]** button.

Type *Ineligible Interest* in the Account Name and Description boxes - then Tab and click **[OK]**.

We will now rename some accounts to better serve our purpose. Do these steps:

Highlight the **Bank Service Charge** account.

Click **Edit**.

Change the Account Name to **Bank / Credit Card Fees** - Tab down to the Description box and change the description to match - click **[OK]**.

Now scroll down to the **Travel Expense** accounts.

Highlight the **Entertainment** account.

Click **Edit**.

Change the Account Name to **Meals & Entertainment** - Tab down to the Description box and change the description to match - click **[OK]**.

Now highlight the **Meals** account - **Edit** - Change the Account Name and Description to **Accommodation**

Hit Tab and click **[OK]**.

Now highlight the **Travel** account - **Edit** - Change the Account Name and Description to **Transportation**

Hit Tab and click **[OK]**.

Note - You will see that you have an expense account, above, for Auto *- use that for expenses that apply to your personal vehicle. The* Transportation *account we just made is for public transit such as buses, trains, taxi rides, etc.*

While we're in this section, highlight the **Meals & Entertainment** account. Now, click the **[New]** icon then type *M&E Sales Tax Expense* in the Account Name and Description boxes.

Hit Tab and click **[OK]**.

Note - the reason for the M&E Sales Tax Expense *account is because when you purchase a meal for business, perhaps to take your editor to lunch, you can only claim 50% of the sales tax on the bill. However, you can still record the other 50% as a straight up expense.*

Okay, now add an **Expense** account for **Advertising & Promotion** because you'll probably spend some money on Facebook ads or AMS promotions to bring attention to your current or future best-sellers.

Since many authors deal with foreign currencies, we're going to need an expense account to capture exchange rate fluctuations. Do this:

Highlight **Expense**.

Click the [**New**] icon and make an account called **Exchange Gain or Loss**

Hit Tab and click [**OK**].

And add one more **Expense** account called **Suspense**. This will be a temporary holding account for transactions that you may need more information in order to post properly, or are uncertain about. The amounts can be reallocated later.

Time to configure the **Income** accounts:

Scroll to the **Income** accounts and highlight **Income**.

Click the [**New**] icon and make an account called **Book Royalties**

Hit Tab and click [**OK**].

Now highlight the **Sales** account and **Edit** to change the name to **Book Sales**.

Note - Book Sales will be for the sales you make from your print book inventory, whereas Book Royalties are for monies you receive from distributors like Amazon or Barnes & Noble.

Scroll to the **Liabilities** account and highlight **Liabilities**.

Click the [**New**] icon and make an account called **Owed to Owner** - make the *Account Type: Credit Card*

Hit Tab and click [**OK**].

Note - this account is for when you spend your personal funds for a business expense. Or when you accidently use the company bank or credit card for a personal purchase.

While the **Liabilities** account is highlighted, let's add another account for **Sales Tax Payable**. This is for the tax you collect on your sales that you have to remit to your local / regional tax agency.

To finish, let's add a couple of **Equity** accounts.

Scroll to the **Equity** account and highlight **Equity**.

Click the **[New]** icon and make an account called **Owner's Equity** - make the Account Type: *Equity*

Hit Tab and click **[OK]**.

Again scroll to the **Equity** account and highlight **Equity**.

Click the **[New]** icon and make an account called **Owner's Draw** - make the Account Type: *Equity*

Hit Tab and click **[OK]**.

With this Chart of Accounts you now have a good listing of the accounts you are most likely to use. We can always add or remove accounts later if need be.

Okay; if you've managed to follow all of the above, then your Chart of Accounts should look like the one listed below. If not, then **Add / Edit / Delete** the necessary accounts to make everything copacetic. Once you list matches mine go get yourself a favourite drink to celebrate - you've done well!

Chart of Accounts

Assets

- Accounts Receivable
- Current Assets
  - Petty Cash
  - Checking Account (or Chequing account, if you prefer - just Edit the name)
  - Savings Account
- Equipment
  - Accum. Depr. Equip.
  - Equipment Purchased
- Inventory

Equity

- Opening Balances
- Retained Earnings
- Owner's Equity
- Owner's Draw

Expenses

- Adjustment
- Advertising & Promotion
- Auto
  - Fees
  - Gas
  - Parking

Repair and Maintenance

Bank / Credit Card Fees

Bank / Credit Card Interest

Ineligible Interest

Cash Discounts

Charity

Cost of Goods Sold

Depreciation

Dues and Subscriptions

Education

Equipment Rental

Exchange Gain or Loss

Insurance

Disability Insurance

Liability Insurance

Workers Comp

Licenses and Permits

Miscellaneous

Office Supplies

Outside Services

Payroll Expenses

Postage and Delivery

Printing and Reproduction

- Professional Fees
  - Accounting
  - Legal Fees
- Rent
- Repairs
  - Building Repairs
  - Computer Repairs
  - Equipment Repairs
  - Janitorial Expenses
- Suspense
- Travel and Entertainment
  - Accommodation
  - Meals & Entertainment
    - M&E Sales Tax Expense
  - Transportation
- Utilities
  - Cable
  - Cell Phone
  - Electric
  - Garbage Collection
  - Gas
  - Internet
  - Phone

- Water

Income

- Book Royalties
- Book Sales
- Interest Income
- Other Income
- Reimbursed Expenses

Liabilities

- Credit Card
- Owed To Owner
- Sales Tax Payable
- Accounts Payable

SETTING UP TAX TABLES

When you get a bill from a vendor or you send an invoice to a customer, more often than not there'll be some sales tax involved. Since sales tax varies from region to region you'll have to configure the program to calculate the correct amount, but this is easily done. Follow these steps:

From the top menu, click on **Business**, then click on **Sales Tax Table**.

On the Tax Table side, click the **[New]** button.

Type in the tax name - where I live we have three main tax rates; *General Service Tax (GST)* which is 5%, *Provincial Sales Tax (PST)* which is 8%, and *Harmonized Sales Tax (HST)* which is 13%.

So, for example, I would type *GST* in the Name box and put 5 in the Value box under Percent.

Then, to choose the account which the tax should post to, click the arrow beside *Liabilities* in the bottom box and scroll down to select **Sales Tax Payable.**

Then click **[OK]**. That window should close and you should see your tax in the left-hand box, and the account it is assigned to in the right-hand box.

To add another tax rate just repeat the above steps.

SETTING UP CUSTOMER PAYMENT TERMS

While we're here, we may as well define payment terms for our customers. Just like your suppliers give you terms (a time period in which to pay), you can do the same with your customers. The three most common terms are *Due On Receipt*, *Net 10 Days*, and *Net 30 Days*. These are used to prompt the customer to pay in a reasonable amount of time. You may have noticed that larger companies will also charge interest on unpaid amounts after the term has expired.

As an author, I have found little need to consider charging interest but the option is there if you wish to pursue it. To minimize delays in payment I set my invoicing to *Due On Receipt.* If it takes a week (or month with large distributors) for the money to get to me then I can live with that, but when bookkeeping for my clients I have found that, when given *Net 30 Days,* customers think they don't have to pay until at least 30 days has gone by - and the staler an invoice gets, the harder it is to collect on.

However, selling to friends or at book signings is an immediate and complete transaction, so *Due On Receipt* is a given.

To set up your terms, do the following:

Click the **Business** icon.

Click **Business Terms Editor**

When the *Terms* window opens click the **[New]** button.

In the New Billing Term - Name box, type *Due On Receipt*

In the Terms Definition - Description box type *Payment due on demand*

Change the Due Days from 30 to 0.

Click **[OK]** to close the window.

Repeat the steps above to make a term called *Net 30* but leave the Due Days at 30.

POSTING OPENING BALANCES

As discussed in the section *Chart of Accounts*, no matter what date you decide to start recording your business transactions, you will be starting with some amounts to be posted in various accounts. These are your Opening Balances. To record them we need to make a Journal Entry.

From the top menu, click **Tools > General Journal**

The *General Journal* register will open.

An empty item line will have the date highlighted. Change this date to the day before your Fiscal Year starts (ie) if you setup the program with your Fiscal Year start date as 01/01/2020, the date you want for this journal transaction is 12/31/2019.

Now, from the icon bar click on **(Enter)**. This will add an item line to the bottom of the register.

Click in the Action box and select Equity.

In the Memo box type *Opening Balance Entries*

Tab over to the Account box and from the dropdown menu choose: Assets:Current Assets:Chequing Account

From your bank statement, put the balance as of the date you have chosen in the `Debit` box (unless your account was in overdraft that day, then put the amount in the `Credit` box).

Tab until a new line appears - you will see the `Debit` amount you put on the previous line now showing in the `Credit` box.

On this new line, again choose Equity in the Action box.

In the Memo box just type the letter *O* and the rest of the description *Opening Balance Entries* should appear.

Tab over to the Accounts box and select Assets:Equipment:Equipment Purchased then Tab to the Debit box and enter the amount of what your office equipment is currently worth.

Now, when you Tab over to the Credit box, you will see that the original amount is highlighted.

Delete that highlighted amount and Tab to get a new line.

Continue to add line items to enter other values that you want to start with like credit card balances, etc.

As we have already seen, each time you open a line a running balance will show in the Credit box. On the final line you will assign this Credit amount to the Equity:Opening Balances account.

When finished, your Debits and Credits should be equal, as below:

Account	Debit	Credit
Assets:Current Assets:Chequing Account	254.65	
Assets:Equipment:Equipment Purchased	1200.00	
Liabilities:Credit Card		132.14
Equity:Opening Balances		1322.51
	1454.65	1454.65

Tab to a new line then click the **[Save]** icon near the top left corner of the screen. Another box will open for you to confirm the Save.

Note - because the Opening Balance Entries were dated before the Fiscal Year, when you Save this transaction it will actually disappear from the Register. However, if you look at the Opening Balances account in the Chart of Accounts window, you will see that the journal entry has been recorded.

For more information on this, see the section, *Opening Balances* in the *Bookkeeping Procedures* section.

ENTERING VENDOR BILLS

Let's say you had a graphic designer do some artwork for the awesome cover of your new book. They send you a bill for $75.00 + tax.

If you haven't entered a bill from this vendor before, you'll need to enter the vendor details:

From the top menu, click on **Business**, then click **Vendor**, then click **New Vendor**.

The window that opens has two tabs: **[Vendor]** and **[Payment Information]**.

In the **[Vendor]** section, fill in the Company Name and the Payment Address details.

In the **[Payment Information]** section, check the box for Tax Table and select the appropriate tax rate as found on the vendor's bills. If the rate doesn't show in your list you will have to add it (see *Setting Up Tax Tables*).

Click **[OK]**.

Now you can enter the bill:

From the top menu, click on **Business**, then click **Vendor**, then click **New Bill**.

In the Bill ID box put the vendor bill (invoice) number.

The Date Opened should be the date the bill was issued by the vendor.

Put the Vendor's name in the Vendor box - if you have already created a vendor file (above) the name should appear when you type the first few letters.

That is all you really need, to move on to the next screen, but feel free to fill in the other fields if necessary.

Now the *Bill Details* page is open you will see that it already shows the information you entered in the previous screen.

In the yellow Description box, detail the product purchased (ie) *new cover for Zero Gravity Cookbook.*

Click in the Action box and select the most appropriate item.

Click in the Expense Account box and select the appropriate expense account - since you probably commissioned an artist to make the new cover above, the expense account would probably be Outside Services.

Enter the number of pieces in the Quantity box.

Enter the price per piece (cost before tax) in the Unit Price box.

Make sure there is an X in the Taxable? box.

I would leave the Tax Included? box blank.

Click in the Tax Table box and select the tax rate the vendor has charged.

Now Tab until a new line appears - at this point you will see at the bottom of the screen the total of the order and a breakdown of the cost and tax amounts.

You can now add another item that was on the vendor's bill, or if everything has been recorded click the **[Post]** icon near the top right corner of the screen.

To close the screen, just click on the **[X]** in the **[View Bill]** tab near the top.

*Note - before you close this screen - IF you paid this bill when you received the product (say you bought some pens at a store), you can record the payment right away by clicking on the **[Pay]** icon at the top right corner of the screen.*

A *Process Payment* window will open.

You will see the Vendor and the bill are highlighted, and the payment amount is filled in.

Make sure that the Date in the Transaction Details section matches the date of the payment.

In the Transfer Account box you will have to click on arrows to select the account where the payment came from (ie) Assets:Current Asset:Chequing Account, or perhaps Liabilities:Credit Card.

Click **[OK]** to finish posting the payment.

IF you happen to pay a vendor bill at a later date, then follow the instructions in the next section:

PAYING VENDOR BILLS

Whenever you pay a vendor, either by cash, cheque, credit card, or e-transfer, you need to record that payment against the vendor's bill. If you didn't pay it immediately (as outlined in the previous section), then you'll need to record the payment, as below:

From the top menu, click on **Business**, then click **Vendor**, then click **Process Payment**.

When the window opens type the vendor name in the top box.

Click on the unpaid bill that appears in the Documents window.

This will populate the Transaction Details and the Amount fields below. Feel free to change the date if the payment is different from what is showing.

In the Transfer Account box you will have to click on arrows to select the account where the payment came from (ie) Assets:Current Asset:Chequing Account, or perhaps Liabilities: Credit Card.

Click **[OK]** to finish posting the payment

Note - if you are using your chequing account and wish to print computerized cheques (instead of writing a cheque out by hand), then check the box for Print Check; *however I'm assuming most authors won't issue that many cheques so I'm not going to spend time detailing that setup - if you wish to go that route, there are instructions in the* GnuCash *software tutorials.*

ISSUING INVOICES TO CUSTOMERS

If you haven't issued an invoice to this customer before, you'll need to enter some customer details:

From the top menu, click **Business**, then **Customer**, then **New Customer**.

The window that opens will have three tabs: **[Customer / Billing Information / Shipping Address]**. Filling in these boxes for each tab is pretty straightforward.

You may need to change the currency shown, and depending on the customer tax may, or may not, check the Tax box and select a rate. Check with your accountant or local tax authority if you aren't sure about this.

Now you can create your invoice:

Click the **[New Invoice]** button on the icon bar.

If the Date Opened is different from the date you want on the invoice, change it.

Enter the customer's name in the Billing Information box - click **[OK]**.

The *Invoice* window will open and you will see it already populated with the customer's name and an invoice number (which will automatically advance each time you create an invoice).

In the line item part of the screen you can change the Date if necessary.

List the item or service in the Description field.

Click in the Action field and select whether you are billing for your time (Hours), book royalties or sales (Material), or some other freelance work (Project).

In the Income field, select the appropriate income account.

Enter the Quantity in the next field.

The cost of the item or service before tax is what you put in the Unit Price field.

The next three fields pertain to any Discount you may be giving. (To keep things simple, I would skip those and just put the discounted price in the Unit Price field).

Make sure there is an X in the Taxable? box if you are charging tax on the item.

Skip the Tax Included box.

Click in the Tax Table box and select the applicable tax rate for the item.

Then Tab. This will not only create a new line for the next item (if there is one) but also total the cost and tax of what you have entered, so far. You will see at the bottom of the screen the Total and a breakdown of the Cost and Tax of the order. *

* Important - always Tab to get an empty line - even if you have no more items - to make sure everything is recorded and you get the correct totals.

If your invoice looks complete, the click the **[Post]** icon at the upper right hand side of the icon toolbar.

Make sure the Post Date and Due Date are correct, then click **[OK]**.

The invoice will remain on the screen but the **[Post]** icon should now be grayed out. Click the **[X]** on the **[View Invoice]** tab to close that window.

Note - before you close this screen - IF the customer paid you at the same time that they received the product (perhaps you were at a book fair), you can record the payment right away by clicking on the Down Arrow next to the Post icon at the top right corner of the screen.

A *Process Payment* window will open.

You will see the customer and the invoice are highlighted, and the payment amount is filled in.

Make sure that the Date in the Transaction Details section matches the date of the payment.

In the Transfer Account box you will have to click on arrows to select the account where the payment should go (ie) Assets:Current Asset:Chequing Account.

Click **[OK]** to finish posting the payment.

IF the customer paid you at a later date (perhaps you left some books at a store to be sold on consignment), then follow the steps in the next section:

RECEIVING PAYMENTS FROM CUSTOMERS

Now, we all get satisfaction from our writing, and it's really nice to get reviews, but nothing beats the feeling of getting paid for our work.

When a customer pays an invoice sometime after they received the product, this is how we record it in GnuCash:

On the top menu, click **Business > Customer > Process Payment**.

When the new window opens type in the customer name - Tab.

In the Documents box you will see any unpaid invoices for the customer.

Select any that are being paid (if you need to select more than one hold down the CTRL key as you click on them).

You will see the payment in the Amount area is the total amount of the invoices you have selected.

If you like you can put the cheque number or confirmation number of the payment in the Num box.

In the Transfer Account box, click the arrow next to Assets then the arrow next to Current Assets then select the bank account where the money is to be deposited.

Click **[OK]** and that's it.

RECONCILING YOUR BANK AND CREDIT CARD ACCOUNTS

When you get your bank or credit card statement use the following steps to make sure your postings match the statement:

The only window you'll need to have open is the *Accounts* window. Close any others.

To reconcile your Bank Chequing account, first make sure it is highlighted in your account list.

From the top menu, click **Actions > Reconcile...**

In the window that opens make sure the Statement Date matches the end date of your bank statement printout.

*The Starting Balance will be 0.00 the first time you do this - that's okay.

In the Ending Balance box enter the balance from your bank statement on the Statement Date.

If the bank has charged or paid you interest, click on the **[Enter Interest Payment]** button.

In the window that opens, enter the interest amount in the Amount box.

In the Date box make sure the date the interest was applied is showing.

In the Payment From box, select the Bank / Credit Card Interest expense account if the bank charged interest, OR the Interest Income account if the bank paid you interest.

Click **[OK]** to close that window, then click **[OK]** to go to the *Reconcile* window.

The *Reconcile* window is divided into two panes: The `Debits` side will show payments that have come out of your bank account. The `Credits` side will show deposits into your bank account.

All you have to do here is click the checkbox for each transaction that matches up to your bank statement.

*The first time you do this you will also have to click the checkbox for the Opening Balance amount.

If everything matches correctly, the Difference in the bottom right corner of the *Reconcile* window should be $0.00.

If you are not showing $0.00 then you need to figure out why before moving on.

If you are showing $0.00 then give yourself a pat on the back and click the **[Reconcile Selection]** icon at the top of the window.

Click **[Finish]** at the top right corner of the window to close it.

Notes:

If a transaction appears on the bank statement that isn't showing in the Reconciliation window, you will need to add it - perhaps you forgot to enter a customer's payment or a cheque you paid to a vendor. Or you may have posted it to the wrong account.

If a transaction appears in the Reconciliation window that doesn't appear on the bank statement, it may be because a cheque you wrote hasn't cleared yet, or you may have posted it to the wrong bank account. If an item hasn't cleared - that's okay - you'll probably pick it up on the next reconciliation.

RUNNING REPORTS

There are six main reports you may want to run to get a picture of your finances for a given time:

Trial Balance - this gives an overview of all of your accounts.

Income Statement - sometime called the Profit and Loss Report - this shows your Revenue and Expenses for a given period.

Balance Sheet - this shows the value of your Assets and Liabilities, and by extension your Equity

Aged Receivables Report - if you have invoiced someone and they have not yet paid you, then the outstanding amount(s) will be in this report.

Aged Payables Report - if you have recorded a bill from a vendor that you have not yet paid, then such amounts will show up in this report.

Sales Tax Report - this will show all of the sales tax that you have collected from customers and paid to vendors. It will also show any remittances you have made to the tax agency or refunds that the agency has sent you.

Trial Balance: Do the following to run this report:

At the top of the screen click on **Reports**.

Click on **Account Summary.**

The report you get will likely be dated for the end of your current Fiscal Year. However, you may want to see how your accounts looked at an earlier time. Do the following to change the report date:

Click on the **[Options]** icon in the toolbar.

Click on **General**.

Click the round button beside Date.

Change the date as required.

Click the **[Apply]** button then click the **[Cancel]** button to close the window.

Income Statement: do the following to run this report:

At the top of the screen click on **Reports**.

Click on **Income & Expense**.

Click on **Income Statement**.

If you need to change the reporting period:

Click on the **[Options]** icon in the toolbar.

Click on **General**.

Click the round button beside Start Date.

Change the date as required.

Click the round button beside End Date.

Change the date as required.

Click the **[Apply]** button then click the **[Cancel]** button to close the window.

Balance Sheet: Do the following to run this report:

At the top of the screen click on **Reports**.

Click on **Assets & Liabilities**.

Click on **Balance Sheet**.

If you need to change the reporting date:

Click on the **[Options]** icon in the toolbar.

Click on **General**.

Click the round button beside Balance Sheet Date.

Change the date as required.

Click the **[Apply]** button then click the **[Cancel]** button to close the window.

Aged Receivables Report: Do the following to run this report:

At the top of the screen click on **Reports**.

Click on **Business**.

Click on **Receivable Aging**.

If you need to change the reporting date:

Click on the [**Options**] icon in the toolbar.

Click on **General**.

Click the round button beside To.

Change the date as required.

Click the [**Apply**] button then click the [**Cancel**] button to close the window.

Aged Payables Report: Do the following to run this report:

At the top of the screen click on **Reports**.

Click on **Business**.

Click on **Payable Aging**.

If you need to change the reporting date:

Click on the [**Options**] icon in the toolbar.

Click on **General**.

Click the round button beside To.

Change the date as required.

Click the [**Apply**] button then click the [**Cancel**] button to close the window.

Sales Tax Report: Do the following to run this report:

At the top of the screen click on **Reports**.

Click on **Reconciliation Report**.

Click the hyperlink ***Edit Report Options***

When the new window opens:

Click the **[Accounts]** tab.

In the Accounts box, click on Assets to highlight it, then use the Down Arrow key on your keyboard to get to Liabilities.

Click the dropdown arrow beside Liabilities to reveal the sub-accounts, then use the Down Arrow key on your keyboard to get to Sales Tax Payable.

Click the **[General]** tab.

In the Report Name box, type *Sales Tax Report.*

In the Start Date dropdown box select the starting date of the period you want the report for (ie) if you want a report for March - choose 03/01/2020.

In the End Date dropdown box select the ending date of the period you want the report for (ie) if you want a report for March - choose 03/31/2020.

Click the **[Sorting]** tab.

In the Primary Key box, select Date.

In the Primary Subtotal for Date Key box, select None.

Click the **[OK]** button at the bottom of the window.

In the icon toolbar, click **[Save Config]** then **[Close]**.

Note 1 - the next time you want this report click Reports > Saved Report Configuration > then select the report. To change the period reported, just click the [Options] icon then the [General] tab, and change the start and end dates.

Note 2 - a slightly odd thing about this report are the column headings Funds In and Funds Out.

Just to clarify, Funds In are tax amounts that you paid on your purchases, whereas Funds Out are the tax amounts you collected from your customers. For more detail on collecting and remitting sales taxes, refer to the Sales Taxes - Recording, Calculating, Filing *section.*

To print any of the above reports click the **[Print]** icon, choose your printer and click **[Print]**.

MAKING BACKUPS

The program is set to automatically backup the data file, which means it creates a copy in case the original file that you work with becomes corrupted. However, this copy is kept in the same directory on your hard drive as the original file. If the directory, or even your hard drive becomes corrupted then no matter how many backups you've made, you will still lose everything.

To protect yourself from this, each time you finish working with GnuCash and close the program, you should copy the data file to an external drive. To do this follow these steps:

Connect the external drive to a USB port on your computer.

Find the GnuCash file icon on your desktop. Right click on that and then click on [Send To].

Select the external drive and the file will be copied for safekeeping. If you get a pop-up window stating 'The destination already has a file of that name' just select **Replace the file in the desination**.

That's it. Spend a few seconds to do this simple process and I can almost guarantee that you'll sleep better at night. Well, at least you won't be worrying about losing your bookkeeping - your plot problems I can't help you with.

GNUCASH RESOURCES

As I alluded to at the beginning of the section, this is by no means a complete tutorial on the use and capabilities of GnuCash. Here are some other resources to assist you:

Click on **Help > Tutorial and Concepts Guide** to access tutorials.

Click on **Help > About**. This opens the *About GnuCash* window which tells you the software version and, more importantly, provides a link to the GnuCash website home page. Here you will find more information and GnuCash-related resources.

Open a web-browser and type *GnuCash* then type your question into Google, Bing, Yahoo, or other search engine. Chances are that someone else has had the same problem you are having and posted it online.

QUICKBOOKS

I started my bookkeeping career when the first computer accounting packages were being developed. While I haven't worked with every package now on the market, I have spent time working with some of the most popular. At the moment, two of the best-sellers on the market are QuickBooks (parent company, Intuit) and Sage. Due to my client base I have subscriptions to both but if I could only choose one of them it would be QuickBooks, hands down.

Before I go on extolling its virtues let me state that, other than using the product, I have no connection or financial interest in Intuit.

There are several versions of QuickBooks, and while none of them are free keep in mind that anything you pay for, to run your business, is an expense you can claim.

For our purposes, I recommend the desktop version of QuickBooks Pro. At the time of writing, the desktop version could be bought for a one time cost of about $300 US, though I did see that Staples was offering a 33% discount. Or you can buy a subscription, directly from Intuit for about $9 US a month. The advantages of the subscription are the lower initial cost, free software updates whenever they become available (usually once a year), and continuous access to support - which can be handy.

Whichever payment package you decide to go with, make sure to specify QuickBooks Pro - Desktop Version. Intuit has several versions of a cloud-based accounting package called QuickBooks Online or QBO, and they are pushing this product extremely hard. While I have clients that use this package, and I am familiar with it, I don't find it as simple or as convenient to use as the desktop version. The main advantage of QBO is that several people can work on it from different locations. The disadvantages for authors, is that the interface is not as intuitive as the desktop version, and there can be time lags for tasks while the software interacts with the cloud. If you don't have a fast and dependable Internet connection, you will really notice the delays.

If you decide to buy QuickBooks directly from Intuit, don't waste your time navigating their website; they go to great lengths to steer potential customers into buying QBO. Just go to the home page, find the sales department phone number (top right of the screen), and talk to a sales rep.

Now, I don't want to reinvent or recreate the wheel, so this chapter assumes that you have made yourself familiar with the basics of the program through the many, many, many tutorials that can be found in the interweb. My intention is to help you to configure the program to the basic needs of an author; that is, I will show you how to make the interface a little less cluttered, and the best ways to do the most common tasks. It may take an hour or two to complete all the steps here but, once you have, these modifications will save you a ton of time later on.

We're going to pick this up at the point where you have already bought or subscribed to QuickBooks Desktop package, and have downloaded the program from Intuit.

INSTALLING QUICKBOOKS

When you click on the downloaded executable file it will open up an *InstallShield Wizard* which will guide you through the installation process, asking you to accept the licence agreement and enter your licence number and product code. Then you will be asked to choose an installation type - choose EXPRESS.

The program will now install on your computer. This takes a few minutes but you will get a 'Congratulations' screen when it is done. Click the button **[Open QuickBooks]**.

On the next screen there will be a button to **[Create a new company]**. When you click that, a window will pop up with a blue button - **[Express Start]**.

When you have clicked that button a new window will open up with some boxes to fill in:

Company Name: Here you will enter the business name you registered. It could be your name or something fancier like AWESOME AUTHOR ENTERPRISES.

Industry: Click the *Help me choose* link beside the box. When the dropdown list appears, select Art, Writing, Photography. This will set up many of the common accounts useful to authors. We'll modify the provided Chart of Accounts, later.

Company Type: This will be Sole Proprietorship, unless you are setting up for a partnership or have incorporated your company.

Note - if you are setting up for a Corporation, then you may have a different fiscal year period than January 1 to December 31, in which case you may be prompted to enter the fiscal year (or the first month of your fiscal year).

*Once you get to the Home screen you can check the fiscal year setting by clicking on **Company** in the top menu bar then **Company Information**. At the bottom of the window that opens you will see the settings for your fiscal year. Change the month if it is incorrect.*

'Tax' Business Number: This is the number that is assigned to your business. If you are not sure about this, contact either your accountant or local tax agency for more information.

Note - you can continue setting up the program without this number, but make sure you get it before issuing any invoices.

Click on the **[Continue]** button.

The next window is where you will enter your address, phone number, email address and website URL (if you have one).

Click the **[Create Company file]** button.

After the program creates the company file, it will show a screen that says, *You've got a company file! Now add your info.*

We're going to skip this step for now - click on the **[Start Working]** button.

CONFIGURING QUICKBOOKS INTERFACE

Here we get our first view of the Quickbooks interface. Although it is one of the nicest you will find in any accounting software, there are a few things we can to make it even more author friendly.

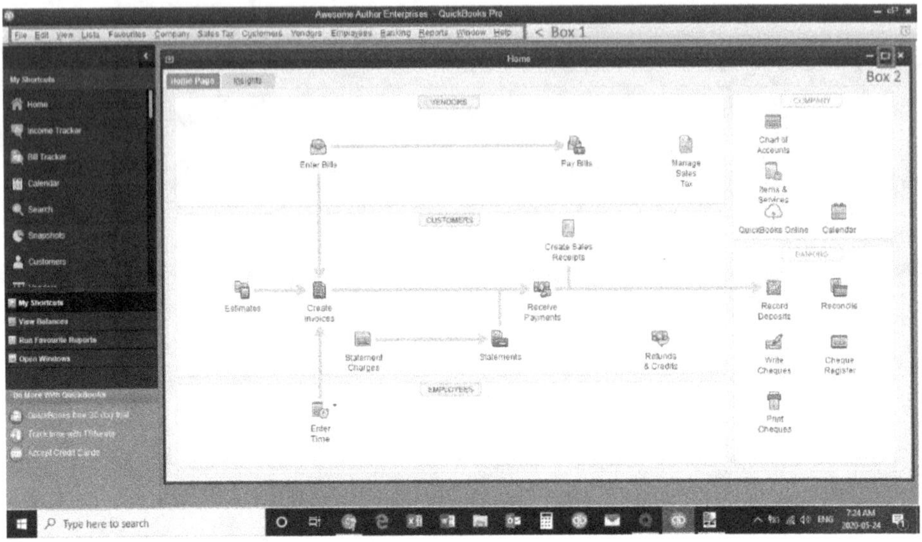

[QB Home Page before modifications]

In the screen shot above, you will see that I have highlighted two areas and labeled them Box 1 and Box 2.

In Box 1, click on **View** and from the dropdown menu click **Top Icon Bar**. You will see that it moved the selection bar, which was on the left, to the top of the screen. This gives us more room to work with.

Now click on the little rectangle inside Box 2 to expand the Home page.

Back to Box 1; click on **Edit** then from the dropdown menu click on **Preferences**. Then from the left side menu click on **Desktop View**.

You will now see two tabs: **[My Preferences][Company Preferences]**.

The **[My Preferences]** tab should be showing but just click on the tab header if it is not. Click the checkbox next to Switch to colored icons / light background on the top icon bar.

While you are in this window, if you want to pretty up the windows, you can also choose a border colour. Click on the dropdown box below COMPANY FILE COLOUR SCHEME and choose a colour that suits you.

Then click **[OK]**.

Alright, now we're going to simplify that top icon bar because there are some icons you won't need and others that we should add.

On the top icon bar, right click in the empty space beside the **[Credit Cards]** icon. A little box will pop up *Customize Icon Bar...* and you should click that box. This will open the *Customize Icon Bar* menu.

Using the **[Delete]** button, delete all the items in the list on the left EXCEPT Home, Calendar, Customers, Vendors, Help. Don't worry if you accidently delete something you meant to keep, it can be added back in.

Now we're going to add a few icons. To do that, click the **[Add]** button to get a list of available icons. The first one we'll add is Back Up Data. Select it and click **[OK]**.

Click **[Add]** again and, just like you added Back up Data, you want to add Calculator, Chart of Accounts, Find Transactions, Memorized Transaction List. When all those have been added, click the **[OK]** button.

There are still a few more handy icons to include but they have to be added a different way, as follows:

From the top menu bar (Box 1), click on **Banking** then **Transfer Funds**. The *Transfer Funds* window will open. Now click on **View** (Box 1) then click on Add 'Transfer Funds Between Accounts' to Icon Bar... then click **[OK]**.

From the top menu bar (Box 1), click on **Company** then **Make General Journal Entries**. The *Make General Journal Entries* window will open. Now click on **View** (Box 1) then click on Add 'Make General Journal Entries' to Icon Bar... then click **[OK]**.

*Note - if you would like to rearrange the icons along the icon bar, just right click an empty space on the bar to get the [Customize Icon Bar...] box, then click on that little box to open the Customize Icon Bar menu. Use your mouse to 'grab' the little diamond beside each item name and you can drag that item, up or down the list, to reposition it. Just remember to click the **[OK]** button to save your changes.*

The screenshot below shows how my *Home* screen looks at this point.

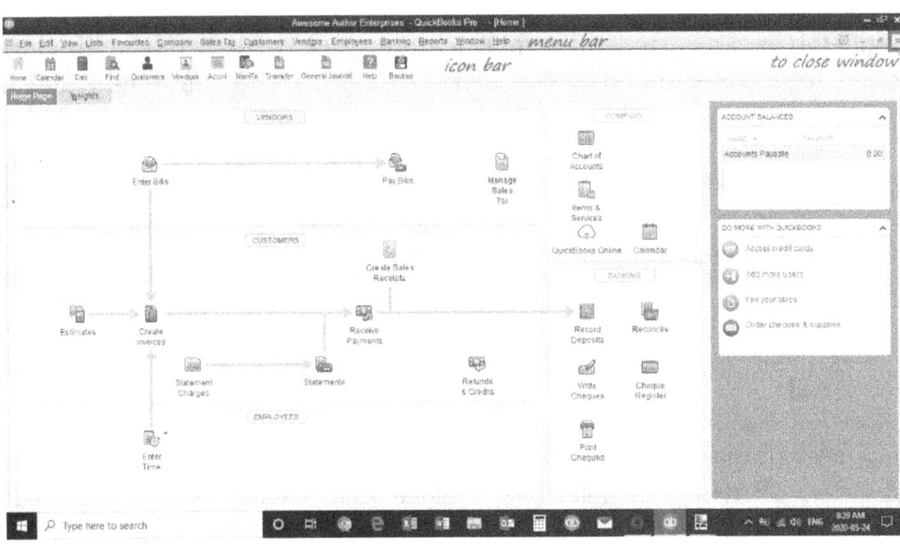

[Modified Home Page Screen]

You'll notice that I have indicated the X to click on to close the window. It is in the gray area below the X in the blue area. As you work you will open various windows and I just wanted to point out that the top X will close the program which you may not want to do.

To shut the program down properly you should click on **File** then **Close Company**. This will shut down the company file and take you back to the company selection screen.

It is possible to use your copy of QuickBooks to create several company files which would be listed here. To shut the program down completely you would again click **File** then **Exit**.

Okay, let's continue with the customization.

On the Menu bar click **Edit** then **Preferences**. In the window that opens you will see a list of functions that you can modify. I will have you click on just a few as follows:

General - [My Preferences] - check the box for Turn off pop-up messages for products and services.

Jobs & Estimates - [Company Preferences] - under Do you create estimates? select **No**.

Multiple Currencies - [Company Preferences] - if you have bank accounts for two or more currencies, meaning that you accept deposits in currencies other than that of your home country, then select Yes, I use more than one currency.

For example, I have a PayPal account for receiving some royalties. In that account, I have some funds in Canadian dollars and some funds in US dollars (PayPal actually keeps these currencies separate). In QuickBooks I will create a USD PayPal bank account that I can use to record any US funds that flows into or out of that account.

The Multiple Currencies function is also useful if you are invoiced in a foreign currency (and you can select from most currencies on the Global market), and you pay via a transfer from your Home Currency. Often, the exchange rate will change between the time you entered the bill and when you paid it. When this happens, QuickBooks recognizes the imbalance and automatically applies the difference to an Exchange Gain or Loss account.

Payments - [Company Preferences] - uncheck the box for Automatically apply payments. Also uncheck the box for Use Undeposited Funds as a default deposit to account.

Payroll & Employees - [Company Preferences] - Click No Payroll.

Sales Tax - [Company Preferences] - if you are not going to charge sales tax on any of your products then select **No** next to Do you charge sales tax? If you will charge sales tax then under Customer and Vendor Tax Codes, select Use Vendor Tax Codes

Time & Expenses - [Company Preferences] - in the Do you track time? box, select **No.** Also uncheck any boxes below that may be checked.

Note - although you may track the time for which you'll charge clients for certain jobs, it is simpler if you track it in a spreadsheet, or other file, and put the hours on your invoice when ready to ask for payment. If you still want to explore QuickBooks' time tracking features, there are good tutorials for this.

SETTING UP THE CHART OF ACCOUNTS

Click on the **[Accnt]** icon on the icon bar to open up the *Chart of Accounts.* We are going to add some accounts, modify a few it did provide, then remove a few that we probably won't use.

First we are going to need some bank accounts:

At the bottom left of the window, click the dropdown arrow next to [Account] to open the menu box.

Select **New**.

In the next window click the button beside Bank then click **[Continue]**

In the Account Name box type *Business Chequing Account*

Click **[Save and New]**

In the Account Name box type *Business Savings Account*

Click **[Save and New]**

In the Account Name box type *Petty Cash*

Click **[Save and New]**

*If you have a PayPal account, or something similar, you can also add that account:

In the Account Name box type *PayPal*

Click **[Save and Close]** when finished entering bank accounts.

When that window closes a pop-up window will appear asking if you want to set-up online banking. Click **[No]**.

You will now be back at the Chart of Accounts screen

At the bottom left of the window, click the dropdown arrow next to [Account] to open the menu box.

Select **New**.

In the next window click the button beside Fixed Asset (major purchases) then click **[Continue]**.

In the Account Name box type *Furn. & Equip. Purchased*

Just below the Account Name box, click the little check box next to Subaccount of, then click the little dropdown arrow and select Furniture & Equipment.

Click **[Save and New]**.

In the Account Name box type *Accum. Depr. Furn. & Equip.*

Just below the Account Name box, click the little check box next to Subaccount of, then click the little dropdown arrow and select Furniture & Equipment.

Click **[Save and New]**.

In the very top box; Account Type click the little dropdown arrow to get the menu, and select Other Current Asset.

In the Account Name box type *Inventory*

Click **[Save and New]**.

In the very top box; Account Type click the little dropdown arrow to get the menu, and select Credit Card.

In the Account Name box type the kind of credit card you will use (exclusively) for your business purchases, along with the last four numbers of the card. For example *Mastercard 1234*

Click **[Save and New]**.

In the Account Name box type *Owed to Owner*. Having this as a Credit Card account is a little hack that will let you easily track and reclaim money you have paid 'out of pocket' for business purchases, or to track and repay the business for personal purchases made with the business bank or credit card

Click **[Save and Close]**.

When that window closes a pop-up window will appear asking once more if you want to set-up online banking. Click **No**.

In the very top box; Account Type click the little dropdown arrow to get the menu, and select Income

In the Account Name box type *Book Sales* (this is for sales of print books from your own stock; the price you sold the books for before any tax).

Just below the Account Name box, click the little check box next to Subaccount of, then click the little dropdown arrow and select Sales.

Click **[Save and New]**.

In the Account Name box type *Book Royalties* (this is for sales of e-books and print books by a distributor; the money the distributor sent you).

Just below the Account Name box, click the little check box next to Subaccount of, then click the little dropdown arrow and select Sales.

Click **[Save and New]**.

In the Account Name box type *Interest Income*

Click **[Save and New]**.

In the Account Name box type *Other Income*

Click **[Save and New]**.

In the Account Name box type *Reimbursed Expenses*

Click **[Save and Close]**.

When you look at the Chart of Accounts now, you will see all of the accounts we have just added. There will be a few more to add but while we're here I want you to modify the Subcontracted Services account.

Click on the Subcontracted Services account to highlight it.

At the bottom left of the window, click the dropdown arrow next to [Account] to open the menu box. Then select **Edit**.

In the very top box; Account Type click the little dropdown arrow to get the menu, and change Cost of Goods Sold to Expense.

In the Account Name box, change Subcontracted Services to Outside Services.

Note - the reason for this change is that you may at some point do subcontracting work, yourself, and I don't want any confusion. Outside Services will be people like graphic designers, editors, or musicians that you hire for a book launch. Also, I want to reserve the Cost of Goods Sold category for reducing your inventory. With that in mind, let's create a Cost of Goods Sold account.

At the bottom left of the window, click the dropdown arrow next to [Account] to open the menu box. Then select **New**.

In the next window click the button beside Other Account Types.

Select Cost of Goods Sold then click **[Continue]**.

In the Account Name box type Cost of Goods Sold.

Click **[Save and Close]**.

Right, let's modify another account.

In the Chart of Accounts, click on the Bank Service Charges (expense) account to highlight it.

At the bottom left of the window, click the dropdown arrow next to [Account] to open the menu box. Then select **Edit**.

In the Account Name box, change Bank Service Charges to Bank / Credit Card Fees. There's no reason why we can't lump those two together.

Click **[Save and New]**.

Now that you know how to add accounts, using **[Save and New]** go ahead and add these Expense accounts:

If you need a refresher on what each account is used for, just review the *Chart of Accounts* section.

Bank / Credit Card Interest

Interest - Ineligible

Licences and Permits

M&E Sales Tax Expense

Printing

Professional Fees - Accounting (make this a subaccount of Professional Fees)

Professional Fees - Legal (make this a subaccount of Professional Fees)

Rentals

Sundry

Travel Accommodation (make this a subaccount of Travel Expense)

Travel Transportation (make this a subaccount of Travel Expense)

Vehicle Fuel

Vehicle Parking and Tolls

Vehicle Repairs and Maintenance

Suspense (Use **[Save and Close]** this time to go back to the Chart of Accounts listing).

We're almost done with the Chart of Accounts. Now we want to declutter it by making *Inactive* the accounts you will likely never use. They can always be made *Active* again if you or your accountant deems them necessary.

Click on Prepaid Insurance to highlight it.

At the bottom left of the window, click the dropdown arrow next to [Account] to open the menu box. Then select **Make Account Inactive**.

Do the same for the following accounts if they appear:

Employee Advances

Accumulated Depreciation

Buildings and Improvements

Land

Leasehold Improvements

Vehicles

Security Deposits Asset

Advance Customer Payments

Payroll Liabilities

Workers Comp. Premiums - Admin

Automobile Expense

Insurance Expense

Payroll Expenses

Rent Expense

Uncategorized Expense

Utilities

Ask My Accountant

If you want to see the accounts you have made *Inactive*, do this:

At the bottom left of the window, click the dropdown arrow next to [Account] to open the menu box. Then select **Show Inactive Accounts**. They will appear with an **x** beside them. To hide the accounts, click **Hide Inactive Accounts**.

Okay, just one more modification and we're done this bit:

Click on the account Computer & Internet Expenses to highlight it.

At the bottom left of the window, click the dropdown arrow next to [Account] to open the menu box. Then select **Edit**.

Change the account name to simply Internet Expenses.

Click **[Save and Close]**.

If you have followed the instructions closely, then your Chart of Accounts should look like the one on the following pages:

Chart of Accounts

Account	Type
Business Chequing Account	Bank
Business Savings Account	Bank
Petty Cash	Bank
PayPal	Bank
Inventory	Other Current Asset
Furniture & Equipment	Fixed Asset
Accum. Depr. Furn. & Equip.	Fixed Asset
Furn. & Equip. Purchased	Fixed Asset
Accounts Payable	Accounts Payable
*Mastercard 1234 (or other name)	Credit Card
Owed To Owner	Credit Card
*Sales Tax Payable (or other name)	Other Current Liability
Opening Balance Equity	Equity
Owner's Draw	Equity
Owner's Equity	Equity
Interest Income	Income
Other Income	Income
Reimbursed Expenses	Income
Sales	Income
Book Royalties	Income
Book Sales	Income

Cost of Goods Sold	Cost of Goods Sold
Advertising and Promotion	Expense
Bank / Credit Card Fees	Expense
Bank / Credit Card Interest	Expense
Depreciation Expense	Expense
Donations	Expense
Dues and Subscriptions	Expense
Education / Workshops	Expense
Equipment Rental	Expense
Interest - Ineligible	Expense
Internet Expense	Expense
Licenses and Permits	Expense
M&E Sales Tax Expense	Expense
Meals and Entertainment	Expense
Office Supplies	Expense
Outside Services	Expense
Postage and Delivery	Expense
Printing	Expense
Professional Fees	Expense
Professional Fees - Accounting	Expense
Professional Fees - Legal	Expense
Rentals	Expense
Repairs and Maintenance	Expense
Sundry	Expense

Suspense	Expense
Telephone Expense	Expense
Travel Expense	Expense
Travel Accommodation	Expense
Travel Transportation	Expense
Vehicle Fuel	Expense
Vehicle Parking and Tolls	Expense
Vehicle Repairs and Maintenance	Expense

If your Chart of Accounts looks like the one above; *Congratulations* - you've done a great job!

SETTING UP ITEMS

One way to speed up the posting of *Invoices* and *Sales Receipts* is to have a list of common items that you sell.

Follow these steps to set up your items:

From the Top menu click on **Lists**, then select **Item List**.

At the bottom left corner of the screen click the dropdown arrow next to [Item].

Select **New**.

A new window will open up with Service highlighted in the TYPE menu.

Here, you want to select Non-Inventory Part.

Note - for things like editing, proofreading, ghost-writing, etc. you would select ***Service*** *from the TYPE menu. For Book Sales or Book Royalties you would select* ***Non-Inventory Part****. (I know you're probably thinking that you'll record the purchase of author copies into your* ***Inventory*** *account, but in this case* ***Non-Inventory Part*** *is the best selection*

In the Item Name/Number box, type in *Book Sales*.

If you have a set price for the item then you can enter it in the Price box. Otherwise, just leave it blank and fill in the price when recording the sale.

Make sure the correct tax code for the item is shown.

Click the dropdown arrow in the Account box and select the appropriate Income account for the item (ie) for Book Sales choose the Book Sale Income account.

Note - you can add an income account on the fly. For example, if you want Ghostwriting to be an item, and would like to have a Ghostwriting Income account then, while you are in the Account box, scroll to the top of the menu until you see <Add New>.

Click on that to open the *Add New Account* window.

Type *Ghostwriting Income* in the Account Name box.

Just remember that Ghostwriting is a Service.

Click **[Save & Close]** to return to the *New Item* screen

When you have filled in all the necessary boxes in the *New Item* screen, click **[Next]** to add another item.

Repeat the above steps to add all of the items you will be selling.

When you have added the last item, click **[OK]** to close the screen.

HANDLING MEALS AND ENTERTAINMENT SALES TAX

As discussed in the *Chart of Accounts* section, whenever you bring home a receipt for a restaurant meal related to a business transaction, you need to split the sales tax. With QuickBooks, you can set up a little routine that will do this for you. The instructions below will show you how:

Note - there are quite a few steps to this but they should only take you ten minutes to complete. This little routine is well worth the time to set up.

Step 1: we'll need to create another tax vendor

Choose **Vendor** from the Top menu bar

Click on **Vendor Centre**

Click the icon for **(New Vendor)** and choose **New Vendor**.

In the Vendor Name box type *Receiver General – Non Taxable* (or the title of whomever you would remit your sales tax to)

Select the [**Sales Tax Settings**] tab

Check the box beside Vendor is a Sales Tax Agency

The Sales Tax Agency box will expand

In the Tax Label box, type *No Tax*

Then check the box for Track tax on purchases separately to

Click the dropdown arrow in the adjacent box and scroll down the list to select **M&E Sales Tax Expense**

Click **[OK]**

Note - a Warning box may pop-op. Click on [Continue Anyway] *to get rid of it.*

Step 2: Now we need to create two sales tax items that make up the sales tax rate. One will be called Eligible Sales Tax - 50%. The other will be called Non-eligible Sales Tax - 50%.

From the top menu bar click on **Lists** then **Item List**

In the bottom left corner of the screen click on [Item]

Select **New**

The Type should be **Sales Tax Item**

In the Sales Tax Name box type *Eligible Sales Tax - 50%*

In the Tax Rate box type *5%* or whatever half of the regular sales tax rate is. For example, the tax rate usually charged on restaurant meals in my area is 13% so I would enter 6.5% in the Tax Rate box

In the Tax Agency box you should be able to select your local tax agency from the dropdown menu.

In the Sales Tax Return box select **Line 106 Input Tax Credits** (your line may vary)

Click **[OK]**

This will bring you back to the *Item List* screen

In the bottom left corner of the screen click on [Item]

Select **New**

The Type should be **Sales Tax Item**

In the Sales Tax Name box type *Not Eligible Sales Tax - 50%*

In the Tax Rate box type whatever half of the regular sales tax rate is, as explained above.

In the Tax Agency box select **Receiver General – Non Taxable**

In the Sales Tax Return box select **Tax on Purchases**

Click **[OK]**

Step 3: Now we need to create a sales tax group

At the bottom left corner of the screen click the dropdown arrow next to [Item].

Select **New**.

A new window will open up with Service highlighted in the TYPE menu.

Here, you want to select **Sales Tax Group**

In the Group Name box type *Meals and Entertainment*

Click inside the box below Tax Item

Click the dropdown arrow to get a list, and choose **Eligible Sales Tax - 50%**

Then click the row below that and select **Not Eligible Sales Tax - 50%**

Then click **[OK]**

Step 4: To link all these together we need to create a Sales Tax Code

From the top menu bar click on **Lists – Sales Tax Code List**

At the bottom left corner or the screen click on [Sales Tax Code]

Then select **New**

In the Sales Tax Code box, type *M&E*

The Description should be *Meals and Entertainment*

Click the button next to Taxable

In the Tax Item for Purchases box, select the sales tax group *Meals and Entertainment*

Click **[OK]**

Close all screens except the *Home* screen.

Step 5: (this is the last step): We need to assign the Sales Tax Code M&E to your Meals and Entertainment account so that the code will automatically apply to all transactions related to meals and expenses.

From the top icon bar click on [Accnt] to open the *Chart of Accounts* screen

Right click on the Meals and Entertainment account to highlight it, and select **Edit Account**

In the Sales Tax Code box, select **M&E**

Click **[Save & Close]** and you're done!

So now, to enter a restaurant receipt, depending on how you paid, click either the [Enter Credit Card Charges] icon or the [Write Cheques] icon on the *Home* screen.

Make sure the correct bank or credit card account is displayed in the top box.

In the Pay To/Purchased From box type the name of the food establishment.

*Note - if you need to add the vendor, in the vendor's [Sales Tax Settings] tab, use **M&E** as the Sales Tax Code, and in the [Account Settings] tab, select the Meals and Entertainment account.*

Put in the receipt date and receipt number.

Put the total receipt amount in the Amount box.

The program should then split the food from the tax, and split the tax into two even amounts.

You'll be happy to know that this concludes the configuration phase. If you need a break this might be a good time. When you are ready we'll get into posting some Opening Balances.

POSTING OPENING BALANCES

As discussed in the *Chart of Accounts* section, no matter what date you decide to start recording your business transactions, it is common to have engaged in business *before* the first day of your bookkeeping. So, one of the first things to record is the state of your business immediately before the first day of your bookkeeping.

You will need to enter:

The value of Assets like any bank balances, and the estimated current value of your equipment, etc.

Liabilities such as funds loaned to you for your business, or credit card amounts on anything you had purchased for your business prior to opening day.

Equity such as money you may have invested to bankroll your business.

Expenses like the value of any office supplies previously purchased.

The sum of these amounts will be considered your Opening Balance, which is essentially what your business is worth on day one.

Note - when making the Opening Balance entries, the date will be the day before the start of your fiscal year. So, if your fiscal year starts on January 1st. then your Opening Balance entries will be dated December 31st. of the previous year. This is so you will have an accurate record of transactions that happened only during the fiscal year, itself.

To record your Opening Balance entries you'll need to make a General Journal entry.

Click on the [GENERAL JOURNAL] icon in the Top icon bar.

In the Date box, click on the little calendar icon to open up the calendar and select the day before the start of your *Fiscal* year. Let's say you want to start tracking your business transactions in 2020, and you have set up your fiscal year as January 1st to December 31st. The date you would choose here is December 31, 2019.

You will now record all the items of value that you are bringing into the business.

Click in the Account box and use the dropdown arrow to bring up a list of accounts. Let's start by selecting your Bank Chequing account. From your bank statement, put the balance as of the date you have chosen in the `Debit` box (unless your account was in overdraft that day, then put the amount in the Credit box).

In the Memo box type, *Opening Balance Entries.*

Click in the next Account box down and use the dropdown arrow to bring up a list of accounts. This time select Furn. & Equip. Purchased. Estimate the current value of any office equipment you have; computers, printers, desks, chairs, lamps, shredders, labellers, etc. and put that amount in the Debit box

In the Memo box *Opening Balance Entries* will likely automatically appear when you Tab over. If not, type it in.

Click in the next Account box down and use the dropdown arrow to bring up a list of accounts. This time select Inventory. If you have any of your books sitting on a shelf waiting for the next book fair or author signing event, figure out the cost (not retail) value of those books (excluding tax) and enter that amount in the Debit box.

In the Memo box *Opening Balance Entries* will likely automatically appear when you Tab over. If not, type it in.

Repeat the above steps to enter any other value you want to start with.

When you have entered all the values, on the last line in the Account box select the Opening Balance Equity account and Tab over until an amount automatically shows up in either the Debit (unlikely) or Credit (most likely) box.

In the Memo box *Opening Balance Entries* will likely automatically appear when you Tab over. If not, type it in.

VENDOR BILLS AND PURCHASE RECEIPTS

Since you will likely have expenses before you get any income, let's look at handling vendor bills and purchase receipts. **The difference between a vendor bill and a purchase receipt is whether you gave payment at the**

time you received the product or service. If you had some proofreading work done, and the proofreader sends you an invoice which you then pay, then that is considered a vendor bill. If you go to Staples, (either in person or online) and purchase some supplies, you would remit payment immediately to complete the transaction. For that you would get a purchase receipt.

Entering Vendors and Vendor Bills

On the *Home* screen click on the [Enter Bills] icon.

In the Vendor box type in the name of the vendor. Hit Tab.

If you have not entered anything for that vendor before a window will open up and notify you that your vendor is not in the vendor list. Click on **[Set Up]**. This will open a *New Vendor* window.

The new vendor name will already be highlighted and the name will also appear in the Address Details - Billed From box. Click below the vendor's name in the Address Details - Billed From box to enter the vendor's address just as you would with any text editor. Also fill any of the other fields in this screen as you feel relevant.

Click on the [**Sales Tax Settings**] tab. In this window click the dropdown arrow in the Tax Code box to select the tax code relevant to the vendor.

Click on the [Account Settings] tab.

Click on the dropdown arrow of the first box and select the account that most closely represents the product or service the vendor provides. For example, if they sent you a print batch of books then choose Inventory (Asset account). If the vendor provided a service, you may want to choose Outside Services (Expense account). If they set up a marquis for your book launch, then perhaps choose Rentals (Expense account).

Then click **[OK]** to accept the vendor settings and get back to the *Enter Bills* screen.

In the Date box select the date on the invoice.

In the Ref. No. box type in the invoice number supplied by the vendor.

In the Amount Due box enter the total amount of the invoice.

Assuming you have set up the vendor details as above, the program will then fill in the fields below for Account, Tax, Amount, and Sales Tax. You can, of course, change the account here, or add more accounts in the rows below.

All you need to do now is type a simple description of what you bought in the Memo box.

Click **[Save and Close]** if you have no more vendor bills to enter, or **[Save and New]** if you want to enter more.

Note - at this point, if you click on the Vendors icon in the icon bar you will see that there is a vendor account for your vendor and it is showing a balance equal to the amount of what you currently owe that vendor.

Also, if you click on the Accnt icon, it will bring up the Chart of Accounts and you will see that the Accounts Payable account now shows the total amount of what you owe your vendor(s).

Entering Purchase Receipts

Which icon you use to enter a purchase receipt will depend on whether you used a debit or credit card, a cheque, petty cash, or your personal cash.

For petty cash, cheque, or debit card; on the *Home* screen click on the [Write Cheques] icon.

A window that looks like a cheque will open up. In the toolbar above it, uncheck the Print Later box.

Make sure that the correct bank account is showing in the Bank Account box. If you paid cash from your petty cash box you would select the Petty Cash account otherwise choose your Bank Chequing account.

In the Pay To The Order Of box, type in the vendor name. If you have not entered anything for that vendor, before, a window will open up and notify you that your vendor is not in the vendor list. Follow the instructions above to enter the vendor into your database.

In the No. box put either the cheque number if you wrote a cheque, or the receipt number on the purchase slip.

The Date should be the date on the purchase slip.

Enter the total amount in the $ box.

If you have set up the vendor details as above, the program will then fill in the fields below for Account, Tax, Amount, and Sales Tax. You can, of course, change the account here, or add more accounts in the rows below.

Note - this section of the screen has two tabs: [Expense] and [Item]. The program should default to the [Expense] tab. This is the one you should use.

All you need to do now is type a simple description of what you bought in the Memo box.

Click **[Save and Close]** if you have no more vendor bills to enter, or **[Save and New]** if you want to enter more.

For personal cash or credit card purchases, on the *Home* screen click on the [Enter Credit Card Charges] icon.

The very top box will show the credit account (e.g.) Mastercard 1234. Make sure this is the correct account. If you used a credit card then select that account. If you used personal cash, then select the Owed to Owner credit card account. This is the reason why we set up Owed to Owner as a credit card account.

In the Purchased From box type in the vendor name. If you have not entered anything for that vendor before a window will open up and notify you that your vendor is not in the vendor list. Follow the instructions above to enter the vendor into your database.

In the Date box enter the date shown on the purchase slip.

Ref. No. should be the transaction or authorization number on the slip.

Put the total cost of the purchase in the Amount box. If you have set up your vendor the program will then fill in the fields below for Account, Tax, Amount, and Sales Tax. You can, of course, change the account here, or add more accounts in the rows below.

Note - this section of the screen has two tabs: [Expense] and [Item]. The program should default to the [Expense] tab. This is the one you should use.

All you need to do now is type a simple description of what you bought in the Memo box.

Click **[Save and Close]** if you have no more vendor bills to enter, or **[Save and New]** if you want to enter more.

Note - at this point, if you click on the [Vendors] icon in the Top icon bar you will see that there is a vendor account for your vendor but it will probably show a $0.00 balance owing. That is because the vendor has been paid.

PAYING VENDOR BILLS

To record the payment of a vendor bill, click on the [Pay Bills] icon on the *Home* screen to get a list of unpaid bills.

Click on the checkbox next to the bill you want to pay.

At the bottom left of the screen select the Date of the payment, the Method*, and the Account.

**If you selected* Cheque *as the* Method *then you need to choose either* To Be Printed *if you have computer cheques, or* Assign Cheque No. *if you write out your cheques manually.*

Click Pay Selected Bills and follow the prompts to either print or assign the cheque.

ENTERING CUSTOMERS, INVOICES, AND SALES RECEIPTS

Much like vendor bills and purchase receipts, whether you issue an invoice or a sales receipt will depend on whether you get paid immediately for your product or service, or sometime after.

Note 1 - if I go to a book fair, I'll take along a little receipt book in case somebody wants a receipt for the purchase of my books. However; unless they specifically ask for one, I don't automatically make one out. They've got the signed book and I've got the cash, so the transaction is complete and everybody is happy. I do, of course, keep track of the sales by writing the purchaser's name on a sheet, usually while I'm asking if they would like to be on my mailing list.

Note 2 - it is a good idea to have a small box, drawer, or file in which you keep any cash or cheques that need to be deposited. Once you make the deposit then you should record the payment using either a Sales Receipt or the Receive Payments function. Do this as soon as possible so there is little chance of forgetting where the funds came from.

Entering Sales Receipts

On the *Home* screen click on the [Create Sales Receipts] icon.

In the Customer:Job box I would type something like *Brant Book Fair May 2020.* Hit Tab.

If you have not entered anything for that Customer:Job before a window will open up and notify you that your Customer:Job is not in the vendor list.

Click on **[Set Up]**. This will open a *New Customer:Job* window.

The new customer name will already be highlighted and the name will also appear in the Address Details - Invoice/Bill To box. It's not really necessary to fill in the address box but you can if you like. Also fill any of the other fields in this screen as you feel relevant.

Click on the [**Sales Tax Settings**] tab. In this window click the dropdown arrow in the Tax Code box to select the tax code relevant to the customer.

Note - keep in mind that book sales may have a lower tax rate in your region.

Then click **[OK]** to accept the settings and get back to the *Sales Receipt* screen.

The Deposit To box should show where you are depositing the funds. This will usually be the Bank Chequing account.

The Date box should have the date of the sale. If not then change it.

The Sale No. box will start at **1** and automatically increment to the next number. If you wish to have a different Sales Receipt number, you can change it.

The Payment Method box is where you would select the type of payment you were given. If you got a cheque, then the Cheque No. box is where you'd record the cheque number.

In the Item box, choose the appropriate item from the dropdown menu - or click **<Add New>** to create a new item.

Type in a Description, put in the Quantity, and the Rate per unit then hit your Tab key.

If you have more items to add then do so otherwise just make sure that the Amount and Tax and Total are all correct, then click **[Save and Close]**.

Note - before you close the screen you can print a copy of the Sales Receipt. I normally wouldn't, however, you can print a copy anytime by retreiving the sales receipt from the customer file and clicking on the [Print] icon.

Back on the *Home* screen you will see on the right hand side an area that displays your money accounts. If you double click on the Business Chequing account it will open the bank register and you will see the money from your Sales Receipt has been recorded in that account.

Entering Invoices

You will usually create an invoice when your product or service is delivered some time before you expect payment.

On the *Home* screen click on the [Create Invoices] icon.

In the Customer;Job box type the name of the customer. Hit Tab.

If you have not entered anything for that Customer:Job before a window will open up and notify you that your Customer:Job is not in the vendor list. Click on **[Set Up]**. This will open a *New Customer:Job* window.

The new customer name will already be highlighted and the name will also appear in the Address Details - Invoice/Bill To box.

Fill in the address box and any of the other fields in this screen as you feel relevant.

Click on the **[Sales Tax Settings]** tab. In this window click the dropdown arrow in the Tax Code box to select the tax code relevant to the customer.

Note - keep in mind that book sales may have a lower tax rate in your region.

Then click **[OK]** to accept the settings and get back to the *Invoice* screen.

The Date box should have the date of the sale. If not then change it.

Click the dropdown arrow in the Terms box.

Select **Due On Receipt**

Note- while it is often common to grant Net 30 terms in business, meaning you are granting the customer up to 30 days from the date of the invoice to pay, I always go with Due On Receipt which means you expect the customer to pay as soon as possible, if not immediately, after receiving your invoice. Experience has taught me that when given Net 30 terms customers will interpret that as not having to pay for AT LEAST 30 days, and with no pressure to pay will toss it in a pile and forget about it. Do not be shy about wanting prompt payment for your hard work. It has value, and if you delivered in a timely manner then you deserve to be paid in a timely manner.

Fill in the boxes on the Item lines the same way as discussed above for *Sales Receipts*, and if you wish to add a message to the customer there are a few felicitations to choose from in the Customer Message dropdown box. Another way to add a message is to use a Description box on a line below the last item. Just click below the last item to open a new line.

When you are happy with the invoice you can click an icon above to send it by [Email], [Print] it, or just **[Save and Close]**.

ACCOUNTS RECEIVABLE

The Accounts Receivable account is an account that QuickBooks automatically creates when it senses the need. Once you have issued an invoice you will then have a receivable, and QuickBooks senses this. If you take a look at your Chart of Accounts you will see the Accounts Receivable account among the Asset accounts, and it should show the accumulative amount of any unpaid invoices.

RECEIVING PAYMENTS

Receiving a payment for an invoice is kind of like getting a Christmas card with money in it. Happy days! Make the deposit then record it in QuickBooks, as follows:

On the *Home* screen click the [Receive Payments] icon.

In the Received From box select the customer who remitted the payment. A list of their unpaid invoices will appear.

Choose a payment method in the Pmt. Method box, and if there is a cheque number you can put that in the Reference # box.

Make sure the Deposit To box is displaying the bank account you deposited the payment to.

In the column with the checkmark, click to select the invoices that are being paid. If the customer has not paid the whole amount then type the adjusted payment amount in the Payment box.

Hit Tab, then if all looks good click on **[Save and Close]**.

Back on the *Home* screen you will see on the right hand side an area that displays your money accounts. If you double click on the Business Chequing account it will open the bank register and you will see the money from your deposit has been recorded in that account.

RECONCILING YOUR BANK AND CREDIT ACCOUNTS

Banks and credit card companies issue statements once a month, so each month you should make sure that what you have posted in your QuickBooks Bank and Credit Card accounts matches what is shown on the statement.

Note - while some institutions issue statements according to a calendar month (ie) May 1st to May 31st, others quite annoyingly use a 30 day period that might start on maybe the 6th or perhaps the 13th of each month.

An odd start date doesn't really affect how you reconcile but, if you want a true picture of your finances for a given calendar month, you will have to reconcile a statement that includes part of the following month. And that means you may have to wait a bit longer, for that statement to arrive, before you can close the month. Not much we can do about that except grumble a bit and carry on.

To reconcile an account, from the *Home* screen click on the [Reconcile] icon.

Make sure the correct Bank or Credit Card account is showing in the Account box.

The Date should be the end date shown on the statement.

The Ending Balance will be the balance on the statement at the end of the period.

Note - if this is the first time you have reconciled the account, the Beginning Balance may show 0.00 even though the statement's beginning balance may be different. Don't worry about that right now.

If the statement shows that you earned interest or were charged bank fees then post the total of those amounts in the respective Interest Earned and/or Services Charges boxes and date them for the end of the calendar month you are closing.

The Service Charges should be posted to the Bank / Credit Card Fees expense account, and the Interest Earned should post to the Interest Income account.

Click **[Continue]** to continue to the *Reconciliation* window.

All payments you have made will be on the left side of the screen, and all of your deposits will be on the right side of the screen.

All you do now is click on the ones that match the transaction amounts in your statement.

If a payment or deposit appears in the statement that you haven't recorded, investigate to make sure it is valid then click on the [Home] icon in the top left corner, and from the *Home* screen do what you need to do enter the missing transaction. Then click on the [Reconcile] icon to go back into the *Reconciliation* screen and click on the added transaction.

Once you have matched up with all the transactions on the statement the Difference amount in the bottom right corner should be 0.00 to show you have reconciled the account.

If the Difference is not 0.00 then you need to look carefully at your statement and screen again. Sometimes it helps to click the **[Unmark All]** button, and start again. When everything is copacetic then click **[Reconcile Now]**. A little window will pop up and you want to select the **Detail** report and click **[Print]**.

Now even though the Difference may be at 0.00 you may still have transactions on your screen that you haven't clicked on. This is okay. Those will be transactions that you have posted but haven't been cleared by the bank, or acknowledged by the credit card company. They will remain unchecked until you next reconcile.

Staple the report to the statement, file it, and give yourself a reward like a chocolate chip cookie or a glass of wine, or both.

REPORTS

There a seven main reports you may want to print on a regular basis. Follow the steps below to print each type of report. For an explanation of each, please refer to the *Bookkeeping Procedures* section.

Trial Balance

From the *Home* screen click on **Reports** on the top menu bar.

Select **Accountant & Taxes** then **Trial Balance**.

Beneath the Home icon, click on the **[Customize Report]** button.

Select the period by choosing the dates in the From: and To: boxes.

Then click on the **[Advanced]** button.

In the Display Rows section click the button beside Non-zero then click **[OK]** to close that window.

Click **[OK]** again to get back to the report screen.

To print, simply click the **[Print]** button above the report.

Profit and Loss / Income Statement

From the *Home* screen click on **Reports** on the top menu bar.

Select Company & Financial then Profit & Loss YTD Comparison.

Note - I like this particular report because it shows your accumulated income and expenses for the year to date, as well as the month you have selected.

Select the period by choosing the dates in the From: and To: boxes.

Click the **[Refresh]** button, then click the **[Print]** button.

Balance Sheet

From the *Home* screen click on **Reports** on the top menu bar.

Select **Company & Financial** then **Balance Sheet Standard**.

Note - since you want your report to be the status of your Assets, Liabilities, and Equity as of a given date (usually the end of a month or year), you will select that particular date in the As Of: box above the report.

Click the **[Refresh]** button, then click the **[Print]** button.

Accounts Receivable Report

From the *Home* screen click on **Reports** on the top menu bar.

Select **Customers & Receivables** then **Open Invoices**.

Select either the end of the month/year or the current date in the date box above the report.

If the report contains any items the click the **[Print]** button.

Note - if any of the invoices on the report have been outstanding for more than 30 days, you should consider sending the customer a statement along with a courteous request for payment.

Customer Statements

You should not let an invoice go unpaid for more than 60 days without having some communication with the customer. Sending a statement along with a polite note is one way to give the delinquent payer a nudge.

From the *Home* screen click on **Customers** on the top menu bar.

In the statement setup window, make the Statement Date either the current date or the last day of the previous month.

Click the button beside Open All Transactions as of Statement Date.

In the Select Customers section below, click the button beside One Customer.

A dropdown box will appear that will allow you choose the customer.

The buttons at the bottom will enable you to **[Preview]** the statement, **[Print]** it, or **[E-mail]** it.

Accounts Payable Report

From the *Home* screen click on Reports on the top menu bar.

Select **Vendors & Payables** then **Unpaid Bills Detail**.

Select either the end of the month/year or the current date in the date box above the report.

If the report contains any items the click the Print button.

Sales Tax Payable Report

This report is usually generated when you need to file your sales tax report with the local agency. The report takes a few steps to set up but can be "Memorized" for later use which will save some time going forward.

From the *Home* screen click on **Reports** on the Top menu bar.

Although you will see **Sales Tax** in the dropdown menu, we are going to choose **Accountant & Taxes** then select **General Ledger**.

Click the **[Customize Report]** button below the **[Home]** icon in the top left corner.

In the From: and To: boxes select the dates that encompass the period for which you want reported.

Near the bottom right corner of the window, click on the **[Advanced]** button.

Click the button beside In-Use button then click **[OK]**.

Now click on the **[Filters]** tab.

In the Account box where All Accounts is showing, click the dropdown arrow and select the *Sales Tax Payable liability account. **Remember this may have a different name.*

Then click **[OK]**.

Now that you can see the report, click on the **[Memorize]** button.

You will be prompted to provide a name for the report. Call it something like *Sales Tax Report* then click **[OK]**.

When you want to run this report in the future, rather than going through the steps above to set it up, simply click on **Memorized Reports** in the top menu bar and select the **Sales Tax Report** from the menu. Then all you have to do is change the dates to suit.

Once you have the report on screen you can either Print it or export it to an Excel spreadsheet. For more information on this I will refer you back to the section: *Sales Taxes - Recording, Calculating Filing.*

QuickBooks Resources

As I alluded to at the beginning of the section, this is by no means a complete tutorial on the use and capabilities of QuickBooks. Here are some other resources to assist you:

Within the program, on the top menu bar, click on **Help** to get a selection of tutorials and support.

When you select **QuickBooks Help** you will have a choice of searching the tutorials that came with the software or accessing the **Live Community**.

The tutorials will show you the steps to complete a task but will not give you accounting advice.

The Live Community resources may be a little better with accounting advice, particularly the forums. However, if you use the help line or the chat room at Intuit (the parent company) realize that the software techs are not accountants. Their job is to tell you how the data moves around in the program, fix a bug, or help you to reset the program, find a file, or recover lost information.

A Final Word

As stated in the introduction, this book is not meant to be a comprehensive manual of accounting procedures. It is meant to help you, an author, get over the hurdle of uncertainty that many experience when faced with bookkeeping.

I hope the information provided gives you the confidence to take control of your business finances, which in turn will allow you to concentrate on your writing.

Obviously, I cannot cover every situation that may come your way but help is just a few keystrokes away if you go online. There is a ton of advice to be found using a search engine like *Google*.

Simply type something like *QuickBooks posting government grants* or *Bookkeeping writing off bad debts* and you will find questions like yours answered on forums and websites hosted by accounting professionals. Keep in mind there is often more than one way to record a transaction.

And, finally, don't be shy about reaching out to an actual bookkeeper or your own accountant. That's what they are there for.

Thanks again for purchasing this guide. May your accounts always reconcile and your books all be bestsellers. Now go and build that empire!

About The Author

Always a writer, Glenn Muller became an author of novels and bookkeeper at about the same time. Now, over twenty-five years later he has his own bookkeeping business with many clients, and several books published in the mystery/thriller genre.

A QuickBooks Pro Advisor, he has worked with several accounting software packages and taught many clients how to setup and maintain their financial records.

Glenn Muller is a Canadian who lives in Ontario, Canada, with his wife and furry kids.

Fiction Titles

BOOMERANG - A standalone techno thriller

THE LETTERHEAD AFFAIR - A standalone short thriller

TORQUE - A Fenn & Lareault mystery thriller

JACKLIGHTER COPSE - A Fenn & Lareault mystery thriller

LEAVE THE RUG - A Fenn & Lareault mystery thriller (WIP due 2021)

Non-fiction

SIMPLIFIED BOOKKEEPING FOR AUTHORS

www.ingramcontent.com/pod-product-compliance
Lightning Source LLC
LaVergne TN
LVHW022054200926
848481LV00003B/903
* 9 7 8 1 7 7 7 2 6 7 3 0 8 *